The Worldwide Legacy of Haute Banque

Peter Lang
Bruxelles · Bern · Berlin · New York · Oxford · Wien

Roger Nougaret & Hubert Bonin (eds.)

The Worldwide Legacy of Haute Banque

From 19th to 21st century

Peter Lang
Bruxelles · Bern · Berlin · New York · Oxford · Wien

Edited with the support of *eabh* (The European Association for Banking and Financial History e.V.) & BNP Paribas

This publication has been peer reviewed.

1 avenue Maurice, B-1050 Bruxelles, Belgique
www.peterlang.com ; brussels@peterlang.com

ISBN 978-2-87574-550-7
ePDF 978-2-87574-551-4
ePUB 978-2-87574-552-1
DOI 10.3726/b19489
D/2022/5678/08

Bibliographic Information published by the Deutsche Nationalbibliothek

The Deutsche Nationalbibliothek lists this publication in the Deutsche Nationalbibliografie; detailed bibliographic data is available online at http://dnb.d-nb.de.

CONTENTS

Foreword
A few thoughts on *Haute Banque*

Jacques de Larosière

The *Haute Banque* (or merchant banking) concept that developed in Paris in the first half of the 19th century is interesting for those who are observing the ups and downs of the global banking system of today.

The first thing that strikes me is that *Haute Banque* is not amenable to a precise definition. It takes the art of history and sociology to understand what it really means and covers. And even after such research, the concept remains somewhat vague and difficult to define with precision. In a world of complex regulation in which each activity, each financial product, is the object of detailed prescriptive and comprehensive definitions, we should reflect a minute on the possible advantages of "vagueness" as opposed to extreme precision. I wonder whether innovation has not suffered from increasing sophistication in regulation. Of course, we all know that too much deregulation – that started in the 1980s – was responsible for some of the major weaknesses of the system.

But my point is different. I am interested in understanding how the banks in France in the years of intense – I should say revolutionary – technological changes in the economy, were able to adapt and find new ways to finance exuberant investment needs. *Haute Banque* houses had to invent, to start from scratch. The fuzziness and freedom that presided over the way they operated were probably, at that stage of their development, a crucial element of their success. I am not sure that if a transformation of the economy of the same intensity were to happen today, the accumulated knowledge and prudence of regulators would allow innovations of the magnitude that took place in the years 1800 to 1850. Let us not underestimate the significance and impact of the banking innovations of those years: arranging and financing enormous international infrastructure projects (in particular railways), attracting global savings by developing bond and equity markets, lending to Governments, taking bank participations in industrial ventures…

The second feature of *Haute Banque* that strikes me has to do with persons. More important than the characteristics of the institution itself was the quality of the people who were getting together. Family links were essential. Partners knew each other from childhood and could trust each other as they could be trusted by their partners. That was the secret of *Haute Banque* houses: never associate yourself with people you don't know perfectly and therefore you can't entirely trust.

This explains the family nature of the *Haute Banque* houses of that time. Those institutions kept strong cultural, religious, matrimonial links. Protestant and Jewish banks flourished at the time although religion was never a distinctive criterion. What was important was the personal and family links between partners: it is only in that sense that religion, as a characteristic of a family tradition, could appear. All these traits are in complete contrast with present banks, as we will see later on.

My last point relates to responsibility and capital. *Haute Banque* houses were "*sociétés de personnes*," i.e. not limited liability corporations. The participants in a *Haute Banque* house used to pool all their assets in the bank and were individually and "*solidairement*" responsible on their own wealth for the losses incurred by the company. This feature explains the importance of trust among the "partners" that I have already stressed. It also explains why every partner had to approve individually each decision to invest.

This is obviously a major difference with the "limited" liability concept that developed in the second half of the 19th century, spread into the "investment banks" or "*banques d'affaires*," like Banque de Paris et des Pays-Bas or Banque de l'Union parisienne, and prevails today. One has to understand that, in a way, what I have called the "vagueness" of the *Haute Banque* concept and its freedom of action were the offsetting elements of their unlimited responsibility. The bank was free to act but the bankers could lose their wealth if decisions had been imprudent.

In a way, regulators had no reason to impose capital constraints and obligations on such banks: as long as the assets of the family were sufficient – and that was critically followed and gauged by the *de facto* "club" of merchant bankers of *Haute Banque* – the risks taken were integrally covered by the bankers themselves. What a contrast with the present banking system where the managers of banks are seldom the owners, where prescribed capital is only a very limited part of credit extended to the clients, and where those institutions, since they are too dangerous to fail, benefit from a *de facto* guarantee provided by the Government!

So, in terms of risk management and of the responsibility of bankers, I believe the "*Haute Banque*" concept should be a source of meditation. I would encourage the members of the Basel Committee to organize, along with historians, a seminar on the respective risks and advantages of the *Haute Banque* concept as opposed to the modern highly regulated but anonymous system in which decisions are influenced by short term profit objectives and are, in fact, delinked from direct personal responsibility. The idea is not to go back to 1830, but to look at valuable ways of instilling best practices of the past in present rules.

Introductory speech: The legacy of Geneva's private bankers

Hugo Bänziger

More than two hundred years ago, at the end of the Napoleonic Wars, the name of Henri Hentsch was well-known in Paris' financial circles. With his jolly personality and driving entrepreneurial spirit, Hentsch had built one of the most prominent entity of the *Haute Banque* in Paris which served the French Government as well as wealthy individuals. Hentsch was a typical representative of a group of Protestant bankers who ushered towards a new area of finance and contributed significantly to the modernization of French society and industry. Geneva was small though – about the size of the *Quartier Latin* in Paris. How could people from such a small, almost provincial place, have had such a big influence and leave such a legacy?

As always, a bit of context helps to understand Hentsch's successful career. Only related through his mother to the established circles in Geneva, the young Hentsch learnt early about the town's business. The expulsion of the Huguenots by Louis XIV in 1684 re-established Geneva's fledging trading business. With more than 10 % of the protestant refugees travelling through Geneva and 5,000 staying permanently, the town took back a large junk of the commerce that had migrated to Lyon over the previous century. Watch making, trade finance, silk and cotton manufacturing became Geneva's thriving businesses. With their protestant relatives scattered all over Europe, some Huguenot families started financing trade and offered payment services.

It did not take long for the French kings to notice that bankers from Geneva – the very same who had to leave France in 1684 – could reliably transfer large amounts of silver to the French Allies in Milan and Bavaria during the great coalition wars of the 18th century. From today's perspective, the commissions were enormous. The Geneva bankers charged

10 % of the money transferred. The elegant *hôtels particuliers* in Geneva's old town built by the Lullin, Mallet and Gallatin families testify of the enormous wealth of these 18th century bankers. These bankers had built a network of family members and trusted agents across Europe, developed the knowledge necessary to manage the logistics of money transfer and knew which individual had surplus funds which could be invested. They know how to raise funds. It was a lucrative business. A century later, Henri Hentsch would still make a big fortune as a payment agent for Napoléon's armies in Italy.

His first job, however, was with Picot, Fazy & Cie, the silk factory of a relative. He started working in Geneva, then managed the firm's branch in Lyon. By the age of 26, he was made partner. Due to the revolutionary fever that befell the town, he had to close the Lyon branch and returned to Geneva where local revolutionaries convicted him to a prison sentence. He escaped to Switzerland but returned to Geneva in 1795, when the French Directorate had re-established law and order in France. By that time, people needed jobs and trade had to be re-established. Hentsch opened his first bank the following year and focused on trade finance and wealth management.

Two years later, he teamed up with Jean Gédéon Lombard, a man with perfect connections to the local establishment. The partnership lasted only until 1798 when the two parties split over diverging business ideas. In the same year, France annexed Geneva and it became a French *Département*. Lombard stayed in his hometown catering to the local business. Hentsch noticed the demand for his services in the French capital and moved to Paris. Under the new consul and later Emperor, business prospered. It was the time when Napoléon developed Belgium as France's industrial heart land, the Louisiana purchase was negotiated, the army modernized and professionalized, the Banque de France and the Paris Stock Exchange were established, and the *Code Napoléon* reformed all aspects of law and commerce. France was "*en marche*."

In this fast-moving environment, the talented, 40 years old Hentsch with his many connections throughout Europe, was a man one could do business with. Quickly, he developed a thriving financing business that outpaced his previous operations in Geneva. If we were to measure his success in today's money, he would be a billionaire. His beautiful house "*Mon Repos*" on the shores of Lake Geneva – looking towards the mighty Mont-Blanc and now open to public visitors – is a perfect reminder of his success.

After Napoléon's defeat at Waterloo and the establishment of a new European order by the Congress in Vienna in 1815, Hentsch alternated his stays between Geneva and Paris. Geneva was his family home, but he knew that the real business opportunities were in Paris. The Restoration slowed down the pace of innovation in France and the heavy loss of population during the war was an enormous burden on the economic development. But most of the new institutions Napoleon had created did survive. It took however much longer for them to have the desired impact. In 1850, the *Bourse de Paris* had less than fifty securities listed. It would take Napoléon's nephew, Napoléon III, to dynamize the French economy again.

Despite all this, Henri Hentsch was not deterred. When in Paris, he threw himself into all sorts of activities. He helped to establish the Compagnie royale d'assurances maritimes, we find him in 1818 as founding director of the Caisse d'épargne et de prévoyance, as much as he arranged loans for the City of Paris (1818), Russia (1819) and Spain (1820). Towards the end of his life, the limitations of his business model became apparent though. None of his sons wanted to step into the father's shoes. Upon his death in 1835, the Hentsch bank was split into several successor companies. The partnership model lacked the continuity required by a modern, industrial society.

It fell onto his grandson, Édouard Hentsch (1829–1892), to develop the full potential of the *Haute Banque*. Using his personal and technical skills, the family's network and its capital, Édouard became a partner in Hentsch, Lütscher & Cie in 1857 and associated it with the Parisian bank Hottinguer, Pillet-Will & Cie. France was again in a fever of modernization. New railway tracks were laid down connecting the entire country, heavy industries were developed in the north of France and modern ports opened the country to the world. France became one of Europe's leading industrial nation; French engineering was so creative that the Sultans on the Bosphorus decided to modernize Turkey by adopting the French model. Its impact is still noticeable today: 7 % of Turkish words are of French origin.

There was almost no financial transaction in Paris which Édouard Hentsch did not participate in. He operated very much like London's merchant bankers, introduced new companies to the stock exchange, arranged *ad hoc* loan syndicates, underwrote securities, acted as an exchange and transfer agent, and dealt in precious metals. As his grandfather Henri, he helped creating new financial institutions and saw the

Crédit mobilier and all these banks not as rivals, but as necessary complement to the existing financial institutions. They had the capacity to mobilize smaller funds which Hentsch could not tap. Not surprisingly we find him as one of the co-founders of the Banque de crédit et de dépôt des Pays-Bas in 1863; when the bank became the Banque de Paris et des Pays-Bas in 1872, he became one of its directors. He also chaired the Comptoir national d'escompte de Paris in 1874, which hosts our conference today, France's first international bank with operations in London, Alexandria, San Francisco, Sydney, Melbourne, Yokohama, Shanghai, Calcutta, La Réunion, Bombay, Hong Kong and Saigon.

Hentsch also served in senior executive positions in several other prominent financial institutions. During the krach of 1889, the Comptoir collapsed due to heavy speculation in the copper price though. Édouard Hentsch had to participate in the rescue and lost not only his money but also all his prestigious positions in the financial industry. He died three years later as a poor and lonely man. The broken Comptoir was eventually rescued by a predecessor bank of today's BNP Paribas, the Banque de Paris et des Pays-Bas.

"Bank Hentsch 2.0" illustrated that globally acting banks need larger capital cushions than an individual can contribute. Global Finance had outgrown the model of the *Haute Banque*. Its contributions to banking remain though: the know-how in syndication, listing of shares, public securities offering, financial innovation, global payments, refinancing, and management are all part of modern banking today. And in areas where less capital is required, the successors of the *Haute Banque* still thrive today. The bank I represent, Lombard Odier Darier Hentsch & Cie, not only has a proud history: we also manage CHF 220bn of clients' wealth successfully every single day.

General Introduction

The *Haute Banque* between history, myth, and resilience

Hubert Bonin & Roger Nougaret

So much time has passed since the first banking revolution of the years 1780–1850, during which hundreds of *Haute Banque* houses (merchant banks, *Privat Banken*) have hatched that it might seem inappropriate to once again evoke a model that would seem obsolete in our time of the Third Industrial Revolution and the digitized bank, as if one wished to enter a "museum of the bank."[1]

However, in June 2017, a conference organized by Hugo Bänziger, Olivier Feiertag, Carmen Hofmann and Roger Nougaret brought together historians, archivists and bankers in Paris (on the premises of BNP Paribas themselves inherited from the Comptoir national d'escompte de Paris, near the *Opéra*), within the framework of the European Association for Banking and Financial History (EABH) and in cooperation with banks BNP Paribas and Lombard Odier. Their intention was to determine how this *Haute Banque* still played a role at the beginning of the 21st century and what models of strategy and management methods it maintained.

The aim was to link these present-day analyses with historical studies and to examine the commonalities between the *Haute Banque* of the past and the present. Can we imagine that the actors of the 21st century would mobilize more or less a "legacy" bequeathed by their predecessors of the 19th and 20th centuries? Of course, the EABH conference could

---

1 See a now ancient book: Joseph Wechsberg, *The Merchant Bankers*, New York, Pocket Books, 1986. Stanley Chapman, *The Rise of Merchant Banking*, London, 1984. Reedition, London, Routledge, 2005. Vincent Carosso, *Investment Banking in America. A History*, Cambridge, Harvard University Press, 1970.

not cover all countries and banks; and this collective work, gathering a large part of the proceedings of this conference, could not be exhaustive.

But it is the issues and themes that count, and the interest of that book therefore resides in its questioning by itself. It makes it possible to confront past and present, to compare banks and places, to highlight key players in this history. This introduction therefore aims to weigh the sustainability of the *Haute Banque* concept and the specificity of its business lines within the general history of the money markets.[2]

1. An ever-fascinating story

It is true that several chapters of this collective work plunge back into the depths of the history of banking places, in the wake of dozens of academic books written by reputable colleagues or many "coffee table books" published by banks or institutions as part of institutional commemorations, such as the 330 years of the German Metzler House,[3] Frankfurt's oldest bank, since 1674. This is a far cry from the models of "globalized banking firms" that drive money markets in the 21st century.

This does not prevent the chapter of Lorans Tanatar Baruh from contributing upstream to define the lifestyle and therefore the philosophy of a *Haute Banque* house, in this case Camondo. She insists in particular on the flow of relations and information that this family animated in Constantinople, Vienna and Paris, essentially. The mobilization of available resources in European places at the service of trade, investment in Ottoman securities, private or public, and in real estate assets resulted from this circulation of data, able to build the confidence of institutional and banking investors, and then, downstream, of their clients.

A *Haute Banque* house is a detector of business opportunities and a federator of capitalists ready to invest. The *Haute Banque*, through its modes of organization, thought and life, is still a source of fascination for historians, who constantly question their capacity for resilience, adaptation to market upheavals and flows of financing, on both sides of the Second World War. About the interwar period, a new book of reflections

---

2 See: Youssef Cassis, Richard Grossman & Catherine Schenk (eds.), *The Oxford Handbook of Banking & Financial History*, Oxford, Oxford University Press, 2016.

3 Stefan Ohmeis, *Insights. History and Stories of Bankhaus Metzler and the Von Metzler Family in Frankfurt am Main*, Frankfurt, Metzler, 2005–2006.

appeared in 2018, that of Brian O'Sullivan,[4] after Alain Plessis reflected on the evolution at the turn of the 20th century.[5]

Further upstream, the year 1819 saw the birth in Geneva of the ancestor of the house Mirabaud, which explains that this house commemorated this date in 2019 on its website. The Mirabaud embodied the osmosis between the European squares, between the banks of the Seine and Lake Geneva. Indeed, this family of merchants, from Jean Mirabaud to his son Jacques, had worked between Milan and Geneva since the 1730s before the son of this one, Jacques, was introduced to the bank in Milan from 1801, where he created his own house in 1814, before remaining a sponsor of his successor in 1833–1846.

The roots of the Mirabaud bank – the name of Mirabaud & Cie was adopted in 1910 – are the fruit of the Paccard initiative in 1819: David-Marc Paccard created David Marc Paccard & Cie in Geneva, while his brother Barthélémy Paccard preferred to go to Paris and set up his bank there in 1822, before Henri Mirabaud joined the Paccard-Dreyfus family and took charge of it in 1859 – hence a rich history until the merger of this Mirabaud house with the Banque de l'Union parisienne in 1953,[6] then the second French investment bank behind Paribas and ahead of Banque de l'Indochine and Rothschild.

All the ingredients of the history of the *Haute Banque* are thus intertwined: a capital of commercial and banking skills, interweaving between several family dynasties,[7] European business networks, a constant renewal of the portfolios of knowledge-make, and links within

4 Brian O'Sullivan, *From Crisis to Crisis. The Transformation of Merchant Banking, 1914–1939*, London, Palgrave-McMillan (Springer), "Palgrave studies in the history of finance," 2018.

5 Alain Plessis, "The Parisian Haute Banque and the international economy in the nineteenth and early twentieth centuries," in Youssef Cassis & Philip Cottrell (eds.), *The World of Private Banking*, London, Ashgate, 2010, p. 127–140.

6 See: Isabelle Chancelier, *Messieurs Mirabaud & Cie. D'Aigues-Vives à Paris, via Genève et Milan*, Paris, Éditions familiales, 2001, p. 11–18.

7 See: Michael Lisle Williams, "Merchant banking dynasties in the English class structure: Ownership, solidarity and kinship in the City of London, 1950–1960," in John Scott (ed.), *The Sociology of Elites*, volume 1, *The Study of Elites*, Aldershot, Edward Elgar, 1990. Michael Lisle-Williams, "Merchant banking dynasties in the English class structure: Ownership, solidarity and kinship in the City of London, 1950–1960," *British Journal of Sociology*, September 1984, volume 36, no. 3, p. 333–362.

religious communities. In this way, data transfer nodes on markets and business opportunities have been set up to overcome information asymmetries and to build the necessary capital of confidence.[8]

Since the 1960s, many publications have devoted themselves to reconstructing this "model" of *Haute Banque*. But the whole question is whether it is confined in a historical past, in a stage of economic development, or whether it has been able to endure while reinventing itself in a way by designing specializations able to differentiate it from the models of "deposit banking," "business banking" and "universal banking" that became dominant in the 20th and 21st centuries – and the notion of "private banking"[9] and "family banking"[10] in particular expresses the resilience of these concepts inherited from the historical *Haute Banque*.

2. The intersection between banking revolutions

Yet, beyond historical investigations in the past, and even the memory of the *Haute Banque*, almost every chapter of this book specifies how the legacy of the *Haute Banque* is still alive today, in particular within groups which preserve their specificity and the capital of skills. The legacy of the legacy – or "path dependency" – therefore retains its appeal to the bankers of the present time, and this book must help explain it. How is it that, despite banking revolutions that drive a radical change, the spirit and the core business of the *Haute Banque* are preserved, play a role in the supply of services of bankers, are part of the "business model" financial conglomerates?

---

8 About networking, trust and business history, see Mark Casson, *Studies in the Economics of Trust*, Aldershot, Edward Elgar, 1995. M. Casson, *Information and Organisation*, Oxford, Oxford University Press, 1997. M. Casson, "Entrepreneurial networks: A theoretical perspective," in Michael Moss, Anthony Slaven & Clara Eugenia Nunez (eds.), *Entrepreneurial Networks and Business Culture*, Sevilla, Fundacion Fomento de la historia economica, Publicaciones de la Universidad de Sevilla, 1998, p. 13–28.

9 See: Youssef Cassis, "La banque privée : une entreprise familiale comme les autres ?," in Jean-Paul Barrière, Régis Boulat, Alain Chatriot, Pierre Lamard & Jean-Michel Minovez (dir.), *Les trames de l'Histoire. Entreprises, territoires, consommations, institutions. Mélanges en l'honneur de Jean-Claude Daumas*, Besançon, Presses universitaires de Franche-Comté, 2017, p. 47–53.

10 See for instance: Garret Gunderson, "Tips for setting up your own family bank," *Forbes*, July 21, 2020 [Tips For Setting Up Your Own Family Bank (forbes.com)].

We will begin by taking an example of the integration of the models generated by the first and second banking revolutions, that of a Bordeaux wine trading house, Cruse & fils frères, created in 1820. At the turn of the 20th century, it relied on the establishments born in the years 1850–1860 for its current banking operations. At the same time, however, the family maintained a close relationship with the European *Haute Banque* in the management of its financial assets. These bankers advised it on the purchase of global securities, mixing wisdom for "quiet investments"[11] and modernity through securities issued by companies participating in this first globalization.[12] The Cruse were in correspondence with the market-places of Paris (Heine, Vernes), London (Hambro and Frühling & Goschen), Geneva (Darier), Frankfurt (Gebrüder Bethmann),[13] Hambourg (Warburg, Hesse Newman & Co, L. Behrens & Söhne), Berlin (Mendelssohn, Schickler) or Stockholm (Weylandt).[14]

In the background, the banks resulting from the second banking revolution monopolize corporate banking (discount, overdrafts, long loans), mixing "transactional banking" – based on accounting analysis – and "relational banking" – relying on faithful face to face dialogue – and became the key players in the financial markets, for the issue of securities and their placement among private clients and with institutional investors. However, the *Haute Banque* houses resulting from the first banking revolution retained their fighting spirit, their skills and know-how to maintain and renew their targeted clientele. Moreover, even the new big banks remained faithful to the "spirit of the *Haute Banque*," making sure to develop their departments oriented towards international affairs and the "relationship banking."

In addition to its Department of Financial Studies, which was set up in 1871 and transformed into the Department of Economic and Financial Studies in 1889, Crédit lyonnais[15] set up in 1887 a

---

11 Archives de Bordeaux Métropole, Fonds privé Cruse, 216S 325, March 23, 1910.

12 Marc Flandreau & Frédéric Zumer, *The Making of Global Finance, 1880–1913*, Paris, OECD, 2004.

13 See: Carl-Ludwig Holtfrerich, *Frankfurt as a Financial Centre*, München, C.H. Beck, 1999.

14 Hubert Bonin, *Cruse à Bordeaux (de 1819 à nos jours). L'esprit d'entreprise dans le négoce et le vignoble*, Paris, Les Indes savantes, 2022.

15 Bernard Desjardins, Michel Lescure, Roger Nougaret, Alain Plessis & André Straus (eds.), *Le Crédit lyonnais, 1863–1986. Études historiques*, Genève, Droz, 2002.

"division of the *Haute Banque*," dedicated to cash management and relations with European correspondents, and a foreign affairs division. They merged in 1932 to create the "*Haute Banque* and Foreign Affairs Direction," which continued until 1972, when it became the International Cooperation Affairs Division. The legacy of the "*Haute Banque*" through a century therefore concerned rather the portfolio of relationships and know-how related to relations with international banking places. "The *Haute Banque* direction was one of much importance, a knot of power, first because it was connected worldwide as it managed correspondent banking and the relations with foreign banks, second because it managed negotiations with the bankers on the Paris market-place about big credits and syndicates."[16]

This capital of know-how had first taken shape at the turn of the 19th century when a Europe of the *Haute Banque* had flourished which had allowed each commercial and financial centre to work in osmosis with its sisters. The financing of the wars provoked by the French Revolution and the First Napoleonic Empire had accentuated this dependence on the capacity of bankers to raise funds. But the trade finance through the clearing of drafts and foreign exchange transactions had served as a lever for the growth of the *Haute Banque*.[17] A foundation of networks and skills had thus been deepened for a few decades, in a first step of this

16 Interview by H. Bonin of Marcel Wormser, former head manager of Banque Wormser Frères in the 1950s–1970s, March 18, 2021.

17 See: Geneviève Daridan, *MM. Le Couteulx et Cie, banquiers à Paris. Un clan familial dans la crise du XVIIIe siècle*, Paris, Loysel, 1994. Christian Grand, *Trois siècles de banque. De Neuflize, Schlumberger, Mallet, de 1667 à nos jours*, Paris, E/P/A éditions, 1991. Herbert Lüthy, *Mallet frères et Cie : 250 ans de banque*, Paris, Cujas, 1963. Isabelle Chancelier, *Messieurs Mirabaud et Cie. D'Aigues-Vives à Paris, via Genève et Milan*, Paris, Éditions familiales, 2001. Jean-François Belhoste & Henri Rouquette, *La maison Seillière-Demachy, banque de l'industrie et du commerce depuis le XVIIIe siècle*, Paris, 1977 (published by the bank). Raymond Dartevelle (ed.), *La banque Seillière-Demachy. Une dynastie familiale au centre du négoce, de la finance et des arts, 1798–1998*, Paris, Perrin-Fondation pour l'histoire de la Haute Banque, 1999. Louis Bergeron, *Banquiers, négociants et manufacturiers parisiens du Directoire à l'Empire*, Paris, EHESS-Mouton, 1978. Serge Chassagne, *Veuve Guérin & fils. Banque et soie. Une affaire de famille (Saint-Chamond-Lyon, 1716–1932)*, Lyon, BGA Permezel, 2012. Bo Bramsen & Kathleen Wain, *The Hambros, 1779–1979*, London, Michaël Joseph, 1979. Edna Healey, *Coutts & Co, 1692–1992. Portrait of a Private Bank*, London, Hodder & Stoughton, 1992. Niall Ferguson, *The House of Rothschild. Money's Prophets, 1798–1848*, London & New York, Penguin Books, 1998.

"first banking revolution," that of the structuring of a *Haute Banque* system in Europe, with ramifications in the United States now in addition.

Nicolas Stoskopf's chapter carefully reconstructs the tangle between the "new bank" and "the old bank" in the second half of the 19th century in France. The *Haute Banque* houses are, for many, stakeholders in the creation of deposit and business banks, because they perceived the need for the Parisian place "to change its dimension" in order to remain competitive and above all to help companies to resist European competition. And it shows that a transfer of experience and skills had taken place in favour of the very young corporate culture of public limited companies of the "second banking revolution". That was also the case for Edward Blount (1809–1902), who crossed the stages of investment banking during the first banking revolution – he founded his merchant bank in Paris in 1831, then joining his forces with Charles Laffitte into Charles Laffitte, Blount & Co (1838–1848) – and then jumped into the take-off of the second one, as he contributed to the birth of Société générale in 1864 and presided over it till the turn of the 20th century (1886–1901).[18]

As for Hugo Bänziger, he accompanied Henri Hentsch back and forth between the squares of Geneva and Paris at the beginning of the 19th century. Hentsch would like to remain rooted in Switzerland, with his family. But many houses seem to prefer to crub their development by remaining anchored in their historical terroir, including Lombard Odier, which he helps to create. His entrepreneurial mindset led him to internationalize his public and private debt-holder operations. This justified his permanent establishment in Paris and the creation of his own business house: he thus participated in the restructuring of the French *Haute Banque.* This allowed H. Bänziger to think of Hentsch's indirect legacy in favour of the reflourishing of Swiss *Haute Banque* in the 21st century, thus launching bridges between History and present development, based on portfolios of business and banking culture, altogether traditional and ever renewed.

---

[18] See his memoirs, dating back to 1902: Edward Blount, *Des chemins de fer à la haute banque. Mémoires de Sir Edward Blount, 1830–1900* (edited in French by Robert Fries), Paris, CTHS, 2011. *Memoirs of Sir Edward Blount (1902),* London & New York, Longmans, Green & Co, 1902. Facsimile, Stuart Reed (ed.), Kessinger's Rare Reprints, 2008.

Similarly, when solid banking places in the United States are taking shape, there are wide opportunities to develop a vast financial market in order to support the growth of "modern" companies, in transport or industry, but also in federal public securities. The chapter of David Thomson examines the strategy of the *Haute Banque* houses in the years 1850–1860: from European, they became Transatlantic, moreover on the scale of the whole American continent, as confirmed by the fall of Barings in 1890 following the Argentina's debt crisis.

Federal US bonds then spread to London and then to continental Europe, thanks to the networks woven by the *Haute Banque* houses in the key marketplaces in the United States. D. Thomson shows that German companies, like Bethmann, became excellent intermediaries for this sovereign debt and became partners of North American issuers – and the case of the Seligmans is symbolic of this, on both sides of the Atlantic, just like L. Speyer Ellisen and Speyer & Co. Investors and the financial press in Frankfurt were now becoming familiar with US issues, and the *Haute Banque* was benefiting of this trend. It was "old" in Frankfurt and "new" in New York, but through the same transatlantic family dynasties.

In his chapter, Éric Bussière, as a specialist historian of Paribas (Banque de Paris et des Pays-Bas) and European finance, has little difficulty in confirming that banks of the second banking revolution, like Paribas, owe a lot to the legacy of dynamic *Haute Banque* houses and ready to join the launch of the new banking economy. Their entrepreneurial spirit was not fixed and managed to adapt to the configuration of the Parisian square, in conjunction with German and Dutch bankers.

To the geographical interweaving, inherited from the *Haute Banque* – itself in the wake of European networks woven since the Middle Ages – was added the capitalistic and strategic interweaving – with notably Bischoffsheim, Goldschmidt, Bamberger, Cahen d'Anvers, Hirsch, Hentsch, etc. A transmission of a capital of know-how resulted from these interactions, hence a rapid and powerful take-off of Paribas, followed shortly afterwards by the Banque parisienne (1874), the future Banque de l'Union parisienne (1904) – and that latter associated *Haute Banque* houses Heine, Hottinguer, Mallet, Mirabaud, De Neuflize and Vernes.[19] But the legacy also lied in the recruitment of employers with

---

19 Hubert Bonin, *La Banque de l'Union parisienne (1874/1904–1974). De l'Europe aux outre-mers*, Paris, Publications de la Sfhom, 2011, p. 14–16.

a European culture, such as Emile Ullmann at the Comptoir national d'escompte de Paris – head of foreign affairs in 1890, then first director in charge with financial affairs and general operations in 1902 and also member of the Board in 1905,[20] till 1915–1916 – or Horace Finaly at Paribas.[21]

This dual relationship, both with large banking firms and with the *Haute Banque*, is still relevant today, as shown in several chapters of this book. Despite the power of the concentration movement that drove the money economy and the size of the institutions that structured each market, fleets of medium-sized banks continue to navigate the sometimes turbulent waters of the markets, by resisting speculative squalls.

3. The issue of the long-lasting of the *Haute Banque*

The *Haute Banque* could suffer from a certain handicap: its houses lacked financial surface, which enticed them to pay strict attention to risk taking; sure, this led to leaving room to competing big banks – simply because their capital lagged behind that of big modern banks. But Jean-Yves Mollier analysed the prudence respected by Heine in front of financial proposals. It practiced a cautious analysis of risks and rejected a lot of them: "Many records of the Heine archives are filled with files about 'non achieved issues'. They had been studied, cross-examined, sometimes started, but, rapidly, they had been stopped or the bank had left the syndicate. A few of them had anyway got a successful result, and in these cases, the bank had been badly advised when it refused to concourse; in general, however, the risk was too far-fetched, the guarantees to success seemed weak, and the bank chose to abstain."[22]

Nevertheless, while this prudence and know-how allowed many *Haute Banque* houses to hold on, giant financial and banking centres were structured at the end of the 20th century,[23] which triggered a movement

---

20 See the link: https://histoire.bnpparibas/en/emile-ullmann-the-banker-who-was-too-german-2/ [accessed November 24, 2021].

21 Éric Bussière, *Horace Finaly, banquier, 1871–1945*, Paris, Fayard, 1996.

22 Jean-Yves Mollier, *Le scandale de Panama*, Paris, Fayard, 1991, p. 157.

23 Youssef Cassis, "Londres, New York et la dynamique des places financières internationales, fin XIXᵉ-début XXIᵉ siècles," *Monde(s)*, Presses universitaires de Rennes, 2018/1, no. 13, p. 25–47. Youssef Cassis, *Capitals of Capital. A History*

of interbank mergers.[24] A majority of houses could not resist: they either disappeared or, more often, they joined a group and integrated into their business banking entity. It was the case for several British houses, such as Morgan Grenfell,[25] which was integrated into Deutsche Bank,[26] or Hambros,[27] taken over by French Société Générale, or Kleinwort-Benson by Dresdner Bank: the "clubbish" aspect of the City dwindled in the years 1970s–1990s.[28] The New York market-place itself endured such an offensive from universal banking on investment banking, as when Deutsche Bank purchased Bankers Trust in 1999.[29]

Even in Switzerland and the City, the "private banks" – originating the now commonplace "private banking" qualification – or merchant banks have experienced a varied fate. At the crossroads between the two places in Geneva and London, Coutts had to reduce its sail, suspended its international expansion and sold in 2015 the Swiss subsidiary created in 1987. Its refocusing expressed a strategy of rooting more conducive to its job as a wealth management bank, in a return to its legacy as a *Haute Banque*, a mission assigned to it by its owner, the NatWest Group.[30]

---

of International Financial Centers, 1780–2005, Cambridge, Cambridge University Press, 2006.

24 Franco Fiordelisi, *Mergers and Acquisitions in European Banking*, London, Palgrave-MacMillan, "Studies in Banking and Financial Institutions," 2009.

25 Kathleen Burk, *Morgan Grenfell, 1838–1988. The Biography of a Merchant Bank*, Oxford University Press, 1989–1990.

26 Catherine Schenck, "The acquisition of Morgan Grenfell," in Werner Plumpe, Alexander Nützenadel & Catherine Schenck, *Deutsche Bank. The Global Hausbank, 1870–2020*, London, Bloomsbury Business, 2020, p. 462–483. See also Christopher Kobrak, *Banking on global markets. Deutsche Bank and the United States, 1870 to the Present*, New York, Cambridge University Press, 2008, p. 331–350.

27 Bo Bramsen & Kathleen Wain, *The Hambros, 1779–1979*, London, Michaël Joseph, 1979.

28 David Kynaston, *City of London: A Club No More, 1945–2000*, London, Chatto & Windus, 2001.

29 Catherine Schenck, "The Bankers Trust acquisition, 1999," in Werner Plumpe, Alexander Nützenadel & Catherine Schenck, *Deutsche Bank. The Global Hausbank, 1870–2020*, London, Bloomsbury Business, 2020, p. 517–536.

30 Coutts had joined the National Provincial & Union Bank of England in 1919, and when that latter merged with National Westminster, it became part of the Natwest group. See: Edna Healey, *Coutts & Co, 1692–1992. Portrait of a Private Bank*, London, Hodder & Stoughton, 1992.

In his book's conclusion ("Endgame"), Brian O'Sullivan highlighted the revolution experienced by the *Haute Banque* houses when they were confronted with the glaring shortage of their own funds: "Big Bang in 1986 gave rise to a strategic dilemma for the remaining larger merchant banks. Many of the leading UK merchant banks, including Barings, Hambros, Hill Samuel, Kleinwort, Morgan Grenfell and Warburgs, tried to adopt an integrated business model to compete in the global securities markets. It required significant amount of capital on a much great scale than was available event to the largest of these firms […]. The collapse of Barings in 1995 finally made clear the delusional strategies of a number of the remaining merchant banking houses. The endgame had been played to its conclusions."[31]

The recurring crises that have shaken the first two decades of the 21st century have accentuated the movement of concentration, especially since globalization imposed requirements of competitiveness.[32] Very few *Haute Banque* houses resisted these shocks: over the decades, a majority of the "big names" disappeared.[33] And even the Rothschilds were questioned in France by the nationalization of their main bank in 1982, before the revival of the dynasty in Paris (with two companies) and London.[34] In the United States, the 2007–2008 crisis saw the disappearance

---

31 Brian O'Sullivan, *From Crisis to Crisis*, *op. cit.*, p. 345.

32 Cécile Bastidon-Gilles, Jacques Brasseul & Philippe Gilles, *Histoire de la globalisation financière. Essor, crises et perspective des marchés financiers internationaux*, Paris, Armand Colin, « U », 2010. Dominique Plihon, Jézabel Couppey-Soubeyran & Dhafer Saïdane, *Les banques : acteurs de la globalisation financière*, Paris, La Documentation française, 2006.

33 Jacques Attali, *Sir Siegmund Warburg, 1902–1982. Un homme d'influence*, Paris, Fayard, 1985. Niall Ferguson, "Siegmund Warburg, the City of London and the financial roots of European integration," *Business History*, May 2009, volume 51, no. 3, p. 362–380. Niall Ferguson, *High Financier: The Lives and Time of Siegmund Warburg*, Harmondsworth, Penguin, 2011 (paperback). Ramin Nassehi, "Deconstruction of the high financier: A critical essay on Ferguson's biography of Siegmund Warburg," *Management & Organisational History*, 2014, volume 9, no. 3, p. 314–320. Jehanne Wake, *Kleinwort Benson. The History of Two Families in Banking*, Oxford, Oxford University Press, 1997. Richard Roberts, *Schroders. Merchant and Bankers*, London, MacMillan, 1992.

34 Niall Ferguson, *The World's Banker. The History of the House of Rothschild*, London, Weidenfeld & Nicolson, 1998. Derek Wilson, *Rothschild. A Story of Wealth and Power*, London, André Deutsch, 1988. Beforehand: Bertrand Gille, *Histoire de la maison Rothschild*, Geneva, Droz, 1965 et 1967 (two volumes). Jean Bouvier, *Les Rothschild*, Paris, Fayard, 1967; second edition, Brussels, Complexe, 1985.

of the legacy of Merril-Lynch, Bear Stearns[35] and Lehman Brothers,[36] who had succeeded in metamorphosing by rising to the scale of the business banking profession.

However, Goldman Sachs held on independently,[37] but opened subsidiaries abroad, as in Paris – whereas Lazard federated his three houses in New York, Paris and London and added the Middle East and the Far East.[38] Goldman Sachs itself had previously experienced a "philosophical crisis" internally: its partners had initially refused the transformation into a public limited company and had joined this project only reluctantly. This led to the listing in May 1999 and the change in the statutes of 221 partners, now shareholders among others in their investment banks, even though they still held 60 % of the capital: the spirit of the *Haute Banque* was therefore somehow entertained. But couldn't we presume it has been challenged by this shift from a prominent merchant banking firm? In fact, only 39 of the original partners were still active there as of 2011,[39] a sign of this loss of faithful roots after 130 years of private partnerships. It is because the change of status could often, on each bank, appear as a denial of the legacy of the *Haute Banque.*

Conversely, big investment banks have ever endured the flight of high-end managers who ended rejecting what they perceived as a drift of corporate culture and the abandonment of *Haute Banque* spirits and practices, notably when proprietary trading gathered momentum in the 2000s in New York and London for the sake of maximizing profits and

---

35 Alan Greenberg (with Mark Singer), *The Rise and Fall of Bear Stearns*, New York, Simon & Schuster, 2010. Kate Kelly, *Street Fighters. The Last 72 Hours of Bear Stearns, the Triumphant Firm on Wall Street*, New York, Barnes & Noble, 2010. William Cohan, *House of Cards. A Tale of Hubris and Wretched Excess on Wall Street*, New York, Doubleday, 2009.

36 Peter Chapman, *Lehman Brothers, 1844–2008. The Last of the Imperious Rich*, New York, Portfolio Penguin, 2010. Larry McDonald & Patrick Robinson, *A Colossal Failure of Common Sense. The Story of the Collapse of Lehman Brothers*, London, Ebury Press, 2009.

37 Suzanne McGee, *Chasing Goldman Sachs. How the Masters of the Universe Melted Wall Street Down … and Why They'll Take us to the Brink Again*, New York, Crown Business, 2010. Lisa Endlich, *Goldman Sachs. The Culture of Success*, New York, Touchstone, 1999, second edition 2000.

38 William Cohan, *The Last Tycoons: The Secret History of Lazard Frères & Co*, New York, Doubleday, 2007.

39 Susanne Craig, Ben Protess & Evelyn M. Rusli, "The Goldman Sachs Diaspora," *DealBook-New York Times*, May 16, 2011 [accessed November 24, 2021].

bonuses at the expense of sound risk-taking and the legacy of the identity of their institution. Or already at this time "*boutiques*" were set up as a way to escape this scramble for greed in investment banking like W. R. Hambrecht & Co.[40] John Goslan, head of investment banking at UBS, opened PrinceRidge in 2005, and Peter Salomon, from Lehman Brothers, his own Peter Salomon Co; and a few other merchant banks emerged too at this time (Greenhill & Co, by Bob Greenhill, head of mergers at Morgan Stanley; Evercore Partners, etc.), thus maintaining the historical dualism between bigwigs and agile houses.

One could suggest that the spirit of *Haute Banque* might have been reignited when hedge funds and private equity funds flourished from the 2000s, those latter being involved in the reorientation of the strategy of the companies after taking control of them through IPOs thanks to a flow of investment banking deals.[41] Their leaders were borne by entrepreneurship and their will to assert themselves as "principals" thanks to venture investment.

And a "big" banker argued that the spirit of *Haute Banque* could be maintained even in firms, as told Peter Blanton, a high banker at Credit Suisse: "When the merchant banking team put together a deal, the folks that blessed it had to put some of their own personal capital into is as well as putting their names on the due diligence [official documents of an operation]. It was a policy. There was a sense that without having skin in the game, we were just agents, without a long-term stake in the outcome."[42]

Whatsoever the way of federating some team spirit and sense of responsibility-sharing, several banking giants could/can preserve some legacy of collective way of business life: "One of the most novel proposals for revising Wall Street compensation revolves around an attempt to bring back the spirit, if not the reality, of the era of partnerships when, as Lehman alumnus Peter Solomon recalled, the partners of a big investment banks sat around in one large room, literally or figuratively peering

---

40 Suzanne McGee, *Chasing Goldman Sachs. How the Masters of the Universe Melted Wall Street Down and Why The'll Take Us to the Brink Again*, New York, Crown Business, 2010, p. 35–36, 41.

41 Suzanne McGee, *Chasing Goldman Sachs*, *op. cit.*, p. 117–119.

42 *Ibidem*, *op. cit.*, p. 205.

over each other's shoulders to ensure that their peers weren't taking too many risks."[43]

It turned out, however, that it is possible to reconcile the status of a limited company with the corporate culture of the *Haute Banque*, as the Swiss markets have shown. Because the risks have become much higher due to the expansion and diversification of activities and internationalization, the need for expanded capital has been felt in order to withstand crises, such as the one that caused the Wegelin house's fall in 2012. This explains why Pictet and Lombard Odier (in 2014),[44] Mirabaud – in 2014 for the Swiss bank, while the parent company became a limited partnership by shares in 2013 – and Gonet (2016) became public limited companies, although six houses still retain their limited family partnership status (Bordier, Baumann, E. Gutzwiller, Mourge d'Algue, Rahn & Bodmer, Reichmuth).[45] But they remain far from the big companies since the Mirabaud group employs only 625 employees.

4. The surprise of the current *Haute Banque* spirit bloom

However, to the amazement of analysts – and historians of the present time – this spirit has regained its vitality in the 21st century! Certainly, the giants of finance hold the bar of the business bank: BNP Paribas was for example "named financial adviser of the year for Central and Eastern Europe in the merger market Europe M&A Awards 2020."[46] The "cathedrals of money" of several banking groups dispose of "side aisles" or "little chapels" that revive the legacy of the *Haute Banque*.

Ton de Graaf's chapter analyses how the large Dutch bank that ABN AMRO has become has managed to preserve in Paris its subsidiary NSM Odier, which helps to revive the legacy of the *Haute Banque*. It can draw on its know-how and a corporate culture that has been handed down to it by several houses (De Neuflize, André, Mallet, in particular) since the

---

43 *Ibidem*, *op. cit.*, p. 208.

44 "Pictet et Lombard Odier tournent le dos à deux cents ans d'histoire," *Le Temps*, February 5, 2013.

45 Jean-Jacques Franck, "En Suisse, la banque en famille cède le pas," *Les Échos*, July 25 2016.

46 BNP Paribas website, December 26, 2020.

turn of the 19th century, as their history indicates, before the addition of Schlumberger in 1945, a general merger in 1966 (hence NSM), and the addition of Jordaan in 1980, Demachy-Worms in 1997–1999 and Odier, Bungener & Courvoisier in 2006.[47]

It is because the geography of finance[48] is constantly moving even if great places dominate.[49] The race for gigantism itself gave rise to a renaissance of the core business and philosophy of the *Haute Banque* – as indicated in the chapters by Laure Quennouëlle-Corre and Hubert Bonin. The first determines how the asset management business has revolutionized over the past four to five decades. Financialization of the economy as a whole, but also so-called neoliberal policies States concerned with mobilizing savings and fortunes in the service of public debt financing circuits and companies have paved the way for many financial products and management techniques supported by specialized teams.

Large banking or insurance groups have developed large-scale subsidiaries; but the spirit of the *Haute Banque* has resurfaced thanks to medium-sized asset management companies, often led by their founders or by teams that promote local relationships and above all a "tailor-made" relationship. As for H. Bonin's chapter, he dives into the groups to identify how their growth has developed in the wealth management bank and in the business bank, thus oriented towards the economy of mergers, acquisitions and divestments, or in asset management.

---

47 Olivier Feiertag expresses a different point of view in "La *Haute Banque* et l'histoire, histoire de la *Haute Banque* : De Neuflize, Schlumberger et Mallet après 1945," in Olivier Feiertag & Isabelle Lespinet-Moret (eds.), *L'économie faite homme. Hommage à Alain Plessis*, Geneva, Droz, 2010, p. 325–343. He sees NSM using history to demonstrate a continuity of the *Haute Banque* until now despite its death as a private bank in the 1980s.

48 Hubert Bonin, "La géographie historique de la finance," in Claude Dupuy et Stéphanie Lavigne (eds.), *Géographies de la finance mondialisée*, Paris, La Documentation française, Les Études, 2009, p. 19–34. Hubert Bonin, "Geoeconomics and banking," in Joseph Mark Munoz (ed.), *Advances in Geoeconomics*, Cheltenham UK & Northampton US, Edward Elgar, 2017, p. 217–226. Gordon Clark & Dariusz Wójcik, *The Geography of Finance. Corporate Governance in the Global Marketplace*, Oxford, Oxford University Press, 2007. Olivier Pastré, *La guerre mondiale des banques*, Paris, Presses universitaires de France, 2007. Paul Langley, *The Everyday Life of Global Finance*, Oxford, Oxford University Press, 2009.

49 Youssef Cassis & Éric Bussière (eds.), *London and Paris as International Financial Centres in the Twentieth Century*, Oxford, Oxford University Press, 2005.

In the money business, the groups decentralized themselves somewhat by entrusting trades to specialized subsidiaries, which themselves, within their own group, set up entities whose teams revive a team-based way of working, as close as possible to their clientele, whether in investment banking, wealth management banking or even asset management when it is oriented towards portfolio management in the "unlisted" (private equity).

The internal culture of many of the subsidiaries of these groups maintaining the advisory business remains true to one form of the *Haute Banque*'s legacy, that of sharing information and thinking within the platforms, such as within Goldman Sachs-Paris, established in 1987 after London in 1970: "The corporate culture at Goldman Sachs is unique. Teamwork is at the heart of our daily lives. I was struck by that when I joined the bank. Other companies are probably putting this forward, but it is really the key to our work philosophy at Goldman Sachs. All our bankers, including senior bankers, are accessible and available. In Paris, the whole team is grouped on the same 'floor'. Our analysts rub shoulders with our associates and turn to them without having to worry about hierarchical barriers. Teamwork allows us to stay connected to each other, make the most of our talents and get the best results for our customers."[50] Beyond the self-centered discourse, it is the sign that this branch of the bank expresses to some extent the revival of these practices specific to a "*Haute Banque* culture."

The book *Doing Deals*[51] enhanced for instance "the network nature of investment banking," despite the "consequences of multiple bank relationships" by the customer companies and sometimes "the decline of trust."[52] To remain competitive from the 1980s to 1990s, they had to reinvent their model of practices, to establish refreshed "relationship management,"[53] in the wake of the – one time forgotten – legacy of *Haute Banque*, even if relationship managers have to work intimately with the

---

[50] A managing director, M&A, Investment banking division at Goldman Sachs Paris, website [www.goldmansachs.com/worldwide/france/meet-our-people/anne]. Goldman Sachs has been set up in 1869.

[51] Robert Eccles & Dwight Crane, *Investment Banks at Work*, Boston, MA, Harvard Business School, 1985.

[52] *Ibidem, passim.*

[53] *Ibidem*, chapter 9.

specialists able to ponder data and the trends of market banking, more or less assuming a function of "agency" within the organization.

The international spin-off of many groups is often affected by the creation of establishments which are structured around teams and leaders who maintain, more or less sustainably, a form of partnership and proximity that draw more or less on the legacy of the *Haute Banque*. Thus, when Raymond James Financial, created in 1962 in the United States, established itself in Paris in 1987, its CEO Emmanuel Laussinotte created entities that are as many banking houses, for the management of private clients and employee savings funds, then for the management of assets: "Raymond James Asset Management International was created in an entrepreneurial spirit, with management being a major shareholder in the structure."[54]

Another example of the mobilization of this legacy of the *Haute Banque* is that of the whole business of wealth management bank has reconnected with the relationship bank to adapt to the needs of the "ultra-rich," the HNWI, at the very top, but also to those of the upper and middle-upper classes, hence the revival of counselling practices and "tailor-made." The history of this model can thus live a new stage.[55] This trend is all the stronger as all companies must sharpen and diversify their offer in order to propose products that take into account the "environmental, social and governance criteria" (ESG), which requires a strong capacity for data analysis and renewed insight.

The paradox is that, in times of race to the waist, start-ups bloomed as if bankers felt the need to rebuild a *Haute Banque*, in order to obtain more strategic mobility, managerial responsiveness, attractiveness and differentiation. The advisory bank would reconnect with the "convenience bank." "*Boutiques*" have opened on both sides of the Atlantic, where each banker brings his or her capital of skills, experience and relationships, either after an already long career or after a first step in a major bank: the legacy of the first banking revolution is highlighted in the midst of the third banking revolution… An example is provided

---

54 Former website rjami.com. In November 2021, the Raymond James Asset Management division was acquired by its management and renamed Gay Lussac Gestion; https://www.gaylussacgestion.com/citiwire-raymond-james-ami-devient-gay-lussac-gestion [accessed November 25, 2021].

55 Youssef Cassis & Philip Cottrell (eds.), *The World of Private Banking*, London, Ashgate, 2010.

by Jean-Marc Forneri,[56] who died in January 2021. This "French-style" senior official joined the banking sector in 1994 at the head of the small French business bank Demachy-Worms, heiress of two *Haute Banque* houses; then he chaired the French subsidiary of Credit Suisse First Boston in 1996; finally, he created the "boutique" Bucéphale Finance in 2004 and ran it until 2014.[57]

Having become masters in the art of diversification, some investment banks now act as true "one stop shop" and no longer hesitate to interfere in the small cap universe, at the risk of breaking with the M&A offer to venture on the path of financing advice. The movement towards debt advisory – different from the restructuring activity – was initiated in the 2010's by the merchant banks, with François Guichot-Pérère and Geoffroi de Saint Chamas as pioneers at Lazard, and Vincent Danjoux at Rothschild.

Small entities joined them in the diversification of M&A structures, such as Oddo BHF – with Laurent Bonnin at the head of DCM & debt advisory – and Leonardo & Co after its acquisition by BPCE-Natixis in 2011 and now Natixis Partners. Their job is to guide the client in its choice of financing in the context of a new LBO transaction, a "dividend recap" or an acquisition, or to negotiate the leverage or the terms of a contract.

Missions are proposed by the *boutiques*, for both offensive and defensive reasons. "For a business banker competing for a sales mandate, the provision of financing solutions is often an important component of the service offering, or even essential in certain situations."[58] The offer of financing advice also makes it possible to maintain the sometimes-exclusive link between the business bank and its client, when the latter seeks to finance itself, therefore in the spirit of the *Haute Banque*. "This offer consolidates the relationship with the customer and makes it possible to secure our M&A deals while gaining speed and optimizing conditions."[59]

---

[56] "Le banquier d'affaires Jean-Marc Forneri s'est éteint," *Le Monde*, December 30, 2020.

[57] Aroun Benhaddou, "Debt advisory, la nouvelle norme des boutiques M&A," *Les Échos/Capital Finance*, November 4, 2019.

[58] Pierre-Louis Nahon, managing director, recruited in debt advisory by Alantra in 2017, *ibidem*.

[59] Philippe Guézenec, managing partner by Clearwater International, *ibidem*.

We can thus quote a piece of institutional communication: "Clearwater International has a dedicated European debt advisory team of 25 people with five professionals in Paris. Our missions include also the co-mandate to the sale and purchasing with M&A teams as autonomous mandates for acquisition financing and refinancing."[60]

This dualism does not prevent partnerships and the interlocking between *boutiques* and banking firms in the practice of *Haute Banque* businesses. Large companies seem to want to be supported in their growth and in the restructuring of their assets by both global investment banks capable of driving global change and by small teams providing taylor-made advice, before the intervention of the business lawyers. But a large market has also emerged when many medium-sized companies, in the process of reconversion or accelerating their emergence – such as the famous "unicorns" – need advisory banks to consolidate their position and refine their development strategy.

5. Conclusion

As a result, the *Haute Banque* sparked the first banking revolution and then managed to adapt its strategy, mode of operation and capital of skills throughout the second and third banking revolutions. It remains an original element of the financial world, hence the interest of this collective book. It confirms the key elements that count in the various trades federated under the generic of *Haute Banque*: the art of capturing information between key places, the ability to maintain personal relationships with other bankers and, above all, managers – including now also those of medium-sized businesses – or fund managers. An internationalized culture is of course a fundamental – for example, Mirabaud has offices in Switzerland (Geneva, Basel, Zurich), Europe (London, Paris, Madrid, Barcelona, Valencia and Luxembourg) and the rest of the world (Montreal, Hong Kong and Dubai). A key quality is also a strong and rapid responsiveness, not to mention, of course, the ability to master the changes in economies and markets.

The use of the phone (mobile but secure) or the mail to animate live his network of business correspondents, the know-how to arouse the curiosity of specialized journalists, the art of gathering rumours

60 Laurence de Rosamel, *ibidem*.

and anticipate financial offensives, the detection of fluctuations in the price of securities remain intrinsic qualities of the actors of the *Haute Banque*. They are complemented by the relational capital cemented by sports and/or cultural activities – through corporate sponsorship – leveraging "human capital" traditional, but constantly enriched by new entrants driven by entrepreneurship and ambition – climbing the ranks of relatively few teams and therefore fluid and conducive to promotions.

The sanitary, economic and social crisis will have even more highlighted the requirements of relational banking but by changing the way of work: "Clients will value the contacts that have demonstrated empathy and offered clear information amid so such uncertainty. For those that did well, the relationship will endure for many years to come [...]. Private clients are migrating to on-screen and digital formats, complementing face-to-face contact. They have talked about 'increased pressure' on banks to recognize what is valuable in the human interaction and what can be delivered without it. The mistake many banks make is that assumption that by not delivering in person, the relationship will be valued less by the client. 'It is not really about person, it is about the information and how it is accessed. That is the game changer'."[61]

Despite our insistance on the long-lasting of the practices, culture, and know-how of *Haute Banque*, and the prevalence of big and diversified banking firms, and despite the resilience of "team spirit" in several of their divisions, a few questions have to be raised. First, the absorption of merchant banks by major players could have distorted the conduct and philosophy of these major institutions, particularly German ones (Morgan Grenfell for Deutsche Bank, Kleinwort for Dresdner Bank, etc.). Second, is not the current evolution of compliance and regulation – about insider trading, anti-money laundering, the fight against bank secrecy and tax evasion – an obstacle to what was part of the *Haute Banque*'s strength, that is the discreet intimacy between the client and the banker?

Finally, doesn't the sophistication and hyper-specialization of economic research in the banking practices today put the creation of

---

[61] "PWM/The Banker Private Banking Awards 2020," introduction to the special issue *Global Private Banking Awards 2020*, *The Banker*, November 2020, p. 4.

powerful economic research teams out of the reach of little-sized *Haute Banque* institutions? One could also ponder what remains of the family or denominational organization of the *Haute Banque*, which could entice historians to launch fresh investigations, in particular thanks to oral history.

Part I

The roots of the *Haute Banque*

Chapter 1

The *Haute Banque* and real estate asset management: The case of Camondo

Lorans Tanatar Baruh

In his book *Capitals of Capital: The Rise and Fall of International Financial Centres 1780–2009*, Youssef Cassis provided a wonderful comparative analysis of the international financial centres in several countries through time. Neither this book nor the papers published by Nicolas Stoskopf[1] or Olivier Feiertag[2] on the *Haute Banque* mention the Camondos. However, the Camondo family whose business prospered thanks to the close relations with the Sublime Porte in the Ottoman Empire has entered into the world of *Haute Banque* in Paris after having moved to this city in 1860s.

Nora Şeni and Sophie Le Tarnec extensively studied the life of the Camondo family, also known as the Rothschilds of the East, drawing from the archives kept at the Nissim de Camondo Museum in Paris.[3]

---

1 Nicolas Stoskopf, "Qu'est-ce que la Haute Banque parisienne au XIXe siècle?," paper presented to the conference organized by the Foundation for the history of the *Haute Banque*, 2000.

2 Olivier Feiertag, "La *Haute Banque* et l'histoire, histoire de la *Haute Banque* : De Neuflize, Schlumberger et Mallet après 1945," in Olivier Feiertag & Isabelle Lespinet-Moret (eds.), *L'économie faite homme. Hommage à Alain Plessis*, Geneva, Droz, 2010, p. 325–343.

3 Nora Şeni & Sophie le Tarnec, *Les Camondo ou l'éclipse d'une fortune*, Paris, Actes Sud, 1997. See also: Naim Güleryüz, "Kamondo, Avram," *Dünden Bugüne İstanbul ...*, v. 4, p. 404–405. Moïse Franco, *Essai sur l'histoire des Israélites de l'Empire ottoman depuis les origines jusqu'à nos jours*, Paris, Librairie A. Durlacher, 1897,

This chapter will analyse the Camondo investments in the real estates[4] in Istanbul, particularly focusing on local sources like the Ottoman State Archive and the Ottoman Bank Archive in Istanbul as well as the newspapers and reviews of the time, while also looking at the materials from the museum.

1. Elites business and investments strategy

The intention here is not to go into the details of the family's banking business but rather analyse their investments in the infrastructure projects and urban property in Istanbul. Before we move on, a quick glance at the city's elite that had mainly prospered through financial transactions with the state, will contextualize the Camondo's investments. These individuals, and, later on the administrators of institutions and companies, without contest, had the capitalistic insight to invest in properties with the expectation of an economic return. They often did not exercise political power and operated within the framework of state power, which was beyond their own administration, as studied by historian Eric Hobsbawn;[5] he continued by stressing that even in areas lagging behind in terms of industrialization, real estate was already losing some of its importance.[6] For instance in 1873 in commercial and semi-industrial Bordeaux,[7] it formed 40 % of the estates at the time of death, while in industrial Lille it formed only 31 %. Yet they had the economic power of negotiating with the State or with the municipality in order to undertake the necessary improvements to increase the value of their property. What was the capacity of these actors to intervene in

p. 244–248. Avram Galante, *Histoire des Juifs de Turquie*, Istanbul, Isis, 1985, volume 2, p. 58–60.

4 On properties, see Nora Şeni, "The Camondos and their imprint on 19th century Istanbul," *International Journal of Middle East Studies*, 1994, volume 26, p. 663–675. Nora Şeni, "Des banquiers faiseurs de ville. Les Camondo à Istanbul," in Daniel Panzac (ed.), *Histoire économique et sociale de l'Empire ottoman et de la Turquie (1326–1960)*, Paris, Peeters, 1995, p. 719–729. Emine Çiğdem Tugay & Mehmet Selim Tugay, *Kamondo Han*, İstanbul, Beyoğlu A.Ş., 2007.

5 Eric Hobsbawm, *The Age of Capital, 1848–1875*, London, Abacus, 2001, p. 284.

6 *Ibidem*, p. 291.

7 Along Pierre Guillaume, "La fortune bordelaise au milieu du XIXe siècle," *Revue d'histoire économique et sociale*, 1965, 43, p. 331, 332 and 351.

the state affairs at a local level? How far could the state and its legislation and regulations be manipulated in reshaping the city?

Moreover, this attitude of the high ranking bourgeoisie or of the elite of the capital, though not explicitly mentioned, could be considered as a way of displaying their fortune in this last quarter of the 19th century – a kind of *Belle Époque* – and of inspiring other sections of society by placing their cultural imprint on the urban landscape. Was this urge of displaying wealth and of influencing not only architectural inspiration but also processes of urban reorganization[8] present in the investment decisions made with respect to property? In other words, how much did the desire of creating "a world after its own image,"[9] affect this elite's investment strategies?

A list compiled from the city plans and commercial directories at the turn of the 20th century confirms that, among the biggest investors of the urban property located at the centre of the city were also bankers like Alléons, Baltazzis, Zarifis, Zographos, Camondos, Lorandos and Émile Deveaux, the latter working as administrator at the Imperial Ottoman Bank but yet possessing a vast fortune. Implanted in the 19th-century financial world of Istanbul, these figures had different forms of investments. Even though they were financially more fragile than their European counterparts, within its limits, it can be argued that these people formed the local *Haute Banque* or a "*Haute Banque* of the periphery." The latter three – Camondos, Lorandos and Deveaux – together with the Imperial Ottoman Bank properties represented the 7.27 % of the overall data in terms of the urban space in our sample derived from the Goad's insurance map of 1905. Each of them had strong connections with Parisian *Haute Banque*, however this chapter will focus on the Camondos, the largest land magnate in Istanbul and earliest of its kind.

---

8 See David Harvey, *Paris, Capital of Modernity*, New York, Routledge, 2003, for a detailed discussion on all its facets and on various actors of the urban transformation of 19th century Paris.

9 Karl Marx and Frederic Engels, *Manifesto of the Communist Party*, London, 1848 [http://www.scribd.com/doc/202256/1848-K-Marx-Manifesto-of-the-Commun ist-Party]. See also Eric Hobsbawm, *op. cit.*, p. 64.

2. Early years of Camondos' investments in real estate

Upon his brother's death in 1832, Abraham Salomon de Camondo inherited all the fortune.[10] Taking advantage of his position as private banker to the Grand Viziers Reşid and Fuad Pashas,[11] besides his own financial affairs, he also invested in infrastructural projects and urban property. First a member of the Commission for the Regulation of the City and then an advisor at the Municipal Council of the Sixth District,[12] Abraham Salomon de Camondo bought several plots and erected important buildings in this district[13] with the insight that Galata would gain prominence and further land value.

His real estate empire consisting of eleven *hans*,[14] ten apartment buildings, thirteen houses, eleven plots of land, six shops, a theatre, a farm, a factory in 1889, was the outcome of advances backed by property. As an Austrian and later an Italian subject, Abraham did not have the right to own property in the Empire; he needed to resort to intermediaries for such operations. However, just after the law recognizing the right of property for Ottomans was passed, Camondo, along with his colleagues Aristidi and İspiraki Baltazzi, applied to the government to obtain the right to register property in their names, despite the fact that they were

---

10 Şeni and Le Tarnec, *Les Camondo*, *op. cit.*, p. 27. Galante, "Fouad Pacha et le Comte de Camondo," *ibidem*, volume 6, p. 109–111.

11 Galante, *Histoire des Juifs* … , p. 110. Güleryüz, "Kamondo, Avram," *Dünden Bugüne İstanbul* … , volume 4, p. 404.

12 Steven Rosenthal, "Minorities and municipal reform in Istanbul," in Benjamin Braude and Bernard Lewis (eds.), *Christians and Jews in the Ottoman Empire. The Functioning of a Plural Society*, New York, Holmes & Meier Publishers, 1982, volume 1, p. 376.

13 Ergin, *Mecelle-i Umûr-ı Belediye*, Istanbul, *İ.B.B. Kültür İşleri Daire Başkanlığı Yayınları*, 1995, volume 3, p. 1304–1305.

14 *Han* (khan) was the traditional name given to Ottoman urban structures used as a temporary residence for travelling traders – as *kervansaray* (caravanserai) – or, more often as a large structure divided into rooms, which were rented by settled traders and craftsmen. The mid-nineteenth century *hans* were architecturally speaking, rather different from the traditional Ottoman *hans*, especially in their Western style, but they still preserved the basic function of a *han*, that of providing a large number of rooms for relatively small businesses. Edhem Eldem, *Bankalar Caddesi: Voyvoda Street from Ottoman Times to Today*, Istanbul, Ottoman Bank Banking and Financial History Research and Documentation Centre, 2000, p. 25–26.

of foreign nationality.[15] In an archival document summarizing the matter, it was noted that since these people had faithfully served the State for a long time, they should not be considered as foreigners, and that this exception, which had been granted before in several cases, would conform to the State's dignity.[16] Though it was not known to whom the right of owning property may have previously been granted, the State archive documents show that Abraham Camondo, who first presented the list of his property to the Ministry of Evkaf, received the permission before the Baltazzis, to whom the decree was granted on March 30, 1861.[17]

In a note written by the High Council (*Meclis-i Vâlâ*) to the Ministry of Evkaf in 1858, it was noted that based on the decree, the property registered in the name of intermediaries, was already transferred to the name of Camondo. This, in fact, clarified Şeni's point that there should be an earlier decree than the one mentioned in Galante, which exceptionally allowed the transfer of the property in the name of the grandson of Abraham in 1866,[18] since at that date their investments on property had already reached considerable size.[19] The note described also the limits of the decree and it was added that the High Council would not agree that the property acquired in the coming years be included in the process, even if this fact would cause some difficulties on the sale of the property.[20]

In 1866, having lost first his wife Esther and later his son Salomon Raphael, Abraham Salomon de Camondo decided to hand over his business to his grandsons and renewed his request for the transfer of property. The petition, presented to the Sultan, underlined the fact that his faithful services to the Porte continued and drew attention to his particular devotion to financial affairs and to the Treasury in the last five or six months, requesting the registration of 23 items of property in the name

---

15 BOA, İ.MVL 446–19880, "Baltacı Aristidi ile İspiraki ve Kamanto bâzergânlar uhdesine geçirilecek emlâka dâir," 1277.N.17 (March 29, 1861), doc. 5 dd. 28 Şaban 1277 (March 11, 1861).

16 BOA, İ.MVL 446–19880, *ibidem*, doc. 3 dd. 15.Ş.1277 (February 26, 1861).

17 *Ibidem*.

18 Galante, *Histoire des Juifs* … , volume 6, p. 109.

19 Şeni, *Les Camondo* … , p. 275, footnote 55.

20 BOA, A.MKT.NZD 267–25, "Ecnebi Kamondo'nun başkasının üzerinde bulunan emlâkının kendi üzerine geçirilmesine bir def'aya mahsûs olarak izin verildiği," 1257Ra.19 (October 27, 1858).

of his grandson, on condition that it would not set a precedent for other cases.[21] The Sultan ratified it the following day, and a few days later the decision was communicated to the Ministry of Evkaf for execution.[22]

The list attached to the petition gives us the detail of the oldest property of the family. The *vakıf* property was mostly registered in the name of Abraham Salomon's wife and that of his son Salomon Raphael's wife, Klara binti Yehuda and Ester binti Nissim, respectively. The usual practice of the time was that to own property, women were declared to be Ottoman subjects, even if this was not the case.[23] A note of the Camondos' secretary, Léonce Tedeschi,[24] who travelled from Paris to Istanbul to record the family's properties[25] in 1888, informs us that Klara and Esther had also followed the same procedure – which was called *takıyye* ("*camouflage*") – until the right to own property was granted to foreigners.[26] A few Muslim names, such as Safvet Pasha, Huriye Hanım, Hasan Bey ibni Süleyman, or Armenian names, such as Merzican Canikoğlu,[27] were probably the names of the former owners to whom advances backed

---

21 BOA, İ.MMS 33–1358, "Mösyö Kamando'nun emlâkinden olub da muvâza'âten başkaları uhdesinde bulunan yerlerin büyük torunu Abraham'ın uhdesine geçirilmesi," 1283.Ş.17 (December 25, 1866). Galante comments on this firman based on the documents in the hands of Leon Piperno, the last director of the society, in charge of the management of properties. Galante, *Histoire des Juifs* … , volume 6, p 109.

22 BOA, A.MKT.MHM 371–66, "Kamanto'nun emlâkından ba'zılarının torunu Abraham adına ferâğının yapılması," 1283. Ş. 23 (December 31, 1866).

23 Before the Nationality Law of 1869, foreigners married to Ottoman women registered their property along their wife's or along her relatives' names. For the Alléon and Hava families cases, see Tanatar-Baruh, "The transformation of the 'modern' axis of the nineteenth-century Istanbul: Property, investments and elites from Taksim Square to Sirkeci Station," Unpublished PhD dissertation submitted to the History Department of Boğaziçi University, 2009, Appendix BB. Camondo property: list, plans and photos, p. 55–56.

24 Of Austro-Hungarian nationality, Léonce Tedeschi was assisted during his visit in Istanbul by his brothers Gabriel Tedeschi, Camondo's architect, and Raphaël Tedeschi, working in the Ottoman Public Debt Administration. Tugay & Tugay, *Kamondo Han*, p. 124. *Annuaire oriental, 1889–1890*, p. 344.

25 Şeni, "The Camondos …," p. 666.

26 See the note in the *Archives du Musée de Nissim de Camondo* (AMNC), Notes of Tedeschi on the Camondos property, 1888, p. 71.

27 Tanatar-Baruh, "The transformation of the "modern" axis of the Nineteenth-Century Istanbul …," Appendix BB. Camondo property: list, plans and photos, p. 405–423.

by property were accorded by the Camondos. The registration of all the real estate in his grandson Abraham's name at the Ministry of Evkaf was completed by March 19, 1867.[28]

The 23 different items which formed the oldest core of this real estate empire are listed below: A closer look at Tab. 1 reveals that all Camondo property was located in Galata except for a *yalı*[29] in Yeniköy, a *han* in Mahmud Paşa and a few mansions in Pera. As Şeni argued, most of them were bought or built according to a specific speculative policy,[30] at least for the earlier years.

Tab. 1. An overview over the Camondos' investments in real estate properties in Stamboul in the 1860s

No	Area	Neighbourhood	Address	Category
1	Pera	Asmalımescid	Glavani, 7	Mansion in masonry
2	Pera	Tomtom	Kolonba, 3, 4 (Felek)	2 mansions in masonry
3	Galata	Bereketzade	Felek, 2, 4	Wooden mansion
4	Galata		Hacı Mustafa	Mansion in masonry
5	Galata	Bereketzade	Kamondo, 3	Wooden mansion
6	Galata		Karaköy, 1, 3, 5, 25	Shop in masonry
7	Galata		K Kumbaracı Yokuşu	Land
8	Galata	Yeni Cami	Kürekçiler, 8	Shop in masonry – *gedik*
9	Galata	Yeni Cami	Mertebani, 12, 13, 15	2 shops and a wooden house
10	Galata	Yeni Cami	Mertebani, 5, 7	Mansion in masonry
11	Galata	Yeni Cami	Mertebani, 7, 8	Wooden mansion
12	Galata		Morfelek	Mansion in masonry – half measure of running water (*nısf masura mâ-i lezîz*)

28 BOA, EV 20150, "Mösyö Kamonto'nun malı olan 23 kalem mahaller ile vakıf-larının isimleri ile senedlerin mikdâr ve kayıdları," 1283.Ş.23–1283.Za.13 (December 31, 1866–March 19, 1867).

29 A *yalı* is a house or mansion constructed at immediate waterside and usually built with an architectural concept that takes into account the characteristics of the coastal location.

30 Şeni & Le Tarnec, *Les Camondo …*, p. 33.

Tab. 1. Continued

No	Area	Neighbourhood	Address	Category
13	Galata	Arap Cami	Perşembe Pazarı, 30	Saatçi Han
14	Galata	Arap Cami	Perşembe Pazarı, 22	Shop under Hanson Han
15	Galata	Yeni Cami	Sebut, 11 [Sevud/ Söğüd] or Sion, 1	Shop in masonry
16	Galata		Sebut [Sevud/ Söğüd]	Selanikli Han
17	Galata	Bereketzâde	Voyvoda, 7, 8	Hamam and 2 shops
18	Galata	Yazıcı	Yazıcı, 6	Mansion
19	Galata		Konfomidi, 87 (Yorgancılar?)	Kuyumcu Han
20	Galata	Yeni Cami	Zülfiyar, 13 (Zülfaris?)	*Han*
21	Galata		2, 4, 5	*Han*
22	Stamboul	Mahmud Paşa	Mahmud Paşa, 75	Lüleci Hanı - *gedik*
23	Yeniköy			Mansion with boathouse

Sources: BOA, İ.MMS 33–1358, *op. cit.* and BOA, EV 20150, *op. cit.*

At the time, the municipality's major undertakings focused on the district of Galata.[31] The opening of Karaköy Square in 1858, the demolition of the walls and the filling of the moats in 1864–1865, and the regularization of the streets in the following years gave Galata the necessary impetus for real estate speculation. The Camondo Han (Fig. 1), which still stands today in all its splendour behind the Commission Han, must have been built by the architect Stampa,[32] just after the opening of the square in 1858 (Fig. 2). Camondo's architect Giorgio Stampa was born in 1836 in Istanbul and educated in Italy. In addition to the *hans*, he built for Camondo, the Iranian Embassy at Cağaloğlu, the Italian Hospital

31 The period of the Sixth District Administration (1857–1877) roughly coincided with the prefecture of baron Georges Haussmann (1853–1870) under Napoleon III Paris. Both planned to maintain and regularize the streets and pavements, waterworks, and sewers, to light the streets, to build parks and gardens, and to provide hygiene. Atilla Yücel, "Typology of urban housing in the 19th century Istanbul," translated by Işıl Kurtoğlu in Yıldız Sey (ed.), *Housing and Settlement in Anatolia, A Historical Perspective, Habitat II*, Istanbul, Tarih Vakfı, 1996, p. 305.

32 AMNC, Notes of Tedeschi ..., p. 3. Also Tugay & Tugay, *Kamondo Han*, p. 249.

at Tophane, American Bible House on Mercan Yokuşu, Santo Pacifico Church in Büyükada and Palazzo Corpi at Tepebaşı accomplished with Giocomo Leoni are his important buildings. He was also in charge of the repairs and renovations of the British Embassy in Tepebaşı after the fire of 1870.[33]

Other *hans*, such as the Ibret, Latif (Fig. 3), Yakut (built by Stampa in 1873) (Fig. 4), Selanikli[34] and Saatçi (Fig. 5) *hans*, were dispersed in the main commercial axis circumscribed between Karaköy square and Perşembe Pazarı, at a few minutes' distance from the harbour and from the bridge that was renewed in 1863 (Fig. 6).[35] This commercial area was modernized to a large extent, but still preserved a few wooden houses on its streets.[36] The only Camondo property on the other side of the Golden Horn, the Lüleci Han was also well located in Stamboul, today's Eminönü (Fig. 7). Surrounded by four streets, the building constituted a block in itself. In Léonce Tedeschi's words, "at a distance of eight minutes from the bridge [Lüleci Han] was at the heart of the commercial district of Stamboul."[37]

As for the Camondo mansions, they were installed in the older residential section of Galata (Fig. 8), extending from Voyvoda Street to the Galata Tower.[38] Wooden houses on Felek, Camondo, Morfelek and

---

33 Cengiz Can, "Levantine architects in post-Tanzimat Istanbul architecture," in *Convegno "Architettura e architetti italiani ad Istanbul tra il XIX e il XX secolo"* by IFEA, IIC and Mimar Sinan University, Istanbul, 27–28 November, 1995, p. 55–60; here p. 55. Yıldız Salman, "Stampa, Giorgio," *Eczacıbaşı Sanat Ansiklopedisi*, Istanbul, YEM, 1991, volume 3, p. 1694.

34 According to the *Journal de Constantinople* issued on April 17, 1862, the Selanik Han was among the newly erected *hans* which would be soon completed. The *han* was described as distinctive for its solidity and elegance, the interior court was covered by a roof made of glass and the galeries as well as the stairs were made of cast iron. Quoted from Öncel, "Un nouveau type d'habitat ...," vol. 2, p. 555.

35 Lorans Tanatar Baruh, "The transformation of the "modern" axis of the nineteenth-century Istanbul ...," Appendix BB. Camondo property: List, plans and photos, p. 405–423.

36 See the above list.

37 Léonce Tedeshi, who in 1888 travelled from Paris to Istanbul with the young Moïse, son of Nissim de Camondo, recorded the property in his small notebook which is now in the archives of Nissim de Camondo Museum. For its Turkish translation see Tugay & Tugay, *Kamondo Han*, p. 250.

38 This is the area named as Galata-Pera in Tanatar Baruh, "The transformation of the "modern" axis of the nineteenth-century Istanbul ..." Appendix BB. Camondo property: List, plans and photos, p. 405–423.

Hacı Ali streets housed the different branches of the family. Moïse, who accompanied Tedeschi in his travels, was probably the last Camondo to have been born in Galata, in the family mansion located on Felek Street, just before the family left for Paris in 1867. Two years later, their grandfather Salomon followed them. One of the reasons for their departure from the city was a desire to better compete for the credits and advances proposed to the government from European market-places. However, the family didn't suspend their affairs in Istanbul. The Isaac Camondo & Cie Bank would continue to function,[39] and so would their investments in property.

3. Investments to transform the older structures of property

The older structures were gradually transformed and modernized. The wooden mansion on Felek Street (Fig. 9) was thus transformed into an apartment building by Gabriel Tedeschi in 1877[40]; the one on Voyvoda Street with an entrance on Camondo Street was turned into a *han*; the one inherited from the family on Yazıcı Street (Fig. 10) was converted into apartments, just like the one on Polonya Street, both being redesigned by the architect Stampa.[41] New lands were bought on the newly filled moats, particularly in Hendek and Lüleci Hendek streets. The plot on Lüleci Hendek, on which three shops had been built, was well located with a view which could not be obstructed thanks to the steep slope. Tedeschi advised constructing on this property, and although he included accounts relative to this building in his notes, no building bearing the name of Camondo appears on Goad's 1905 map,[42] apparently because the plot was sold before the building's realization.[43]

---

[39] The 1904 trade directory informs us that the company was founded in Paris in 1870 having its offices in Bahtiyar Han, Galata. *Annuaire oriental, 1904*, p. 408.

[40] He lived in Camondo apartment at Yazıcı Street, 42, between 1889 and 1921. Tugay & Tugay, *Kamondo Han*, p. 132. Gabriel Tedeschi's name was still present in the list of inhabitants of the apartment building in 1922. *Ibidem*, p. 154.

[41] AMNC, Notes of Tedeschi ..., p. 14, 17, 18. Tugay & Tugay, *Kamondo Han*, p. 251–252.

[42] AMNC, *ibidem*, p. 26. See also Tugay & Tugay, *ibidem*, p. 254. Goad, no. 35 and 29.

[43] Tugay & Tugay, *ibidem*, p. 128.

Up in the Pera district, three new apartment buildings were built; first, the colossal apartment building located on the plot between Kabristan and Yemenici streets; second, the wooden houses that had been transformed into an apartment building, located on Nane Street in the Ağa Camii neighbourhood, at a two-minute distance from the *Grande Rue de Péra* (Fig. 11),[44] and finally, the prestigious apartment building on that avenue (Fig. 12), at numbers 123 through 127, in the same district, reconstructed after the 1870 Pera fire.[45] A note on the list of title deeds informs us that these new properties were registered under the name of comte Avram de Camondo by an official document of the Italian Embassy,[46] which was probably completed after the ratification in 1873 of the protocol with Italy on the ownership of property by foreigners.

After his father's death, Moïse de Camondo visited the sites with Léonce Tedeschi and established a real estate company in partnership with his uncle Abraham de Camondo in July 1889. They registered 55 items of their urban property[47] under the company, which would administer them and organize construction projects and works on the plots.[48] The company operated in Istanbul for fifty years, and its offices would be located at the I. Camondo et Cie Bank, functioning on the second floor of the Camondo Han in Yorgancılar, Galata.

However, the Camondos' property was not limited to these 55 items. They had set apart their *yalı* in Yeniköy and some other property which, registered under the name of Abraham de Camondo, no longer belonged to the family.[49] Another list comprising property whose revenues were dedicated to charity was also set apart. One half of a shop on Yeni Cami Street and others on Billur, Sevud, Kürekçiler and Mahmud Paşa Streets, houses on Mertebani and Bakır streets, 80 % of Selanikli Han

---

44 AMNC, Notes of Tedeschi ..., p. 16. Tugay & Tugay, *Kamondo Han*, p. 252.

45 Tanatar Baruh, "The transformation of the "modern" axis of the nineteenth-century Istanbul ..." Appendix BB. Camondo property: List, plans and photos, p. 405–423.

46 AMNC, "Recensement des titres de propriété opéré le 8 Avril 1884," translated in Tugay & Tugay, *Kamondo Han*, p. 120–123.

47 See these properties with a reference date 1884 in the list in Appendix BB. Also Tugay & Tugay, *ibidem*, p. 127.

48 Article 5 of the agreement made an elaborate description of the functions of the company.

49 AMNC, Contract related to the foundation of the real estate company, Constantinople, July 1, 1899. See Article 2.

on Zülfarisse Street and finally the school in Hasköy named after the family were mentioned in the appendix of the contract, specifying that their revenues would continue to be donated to the allocate recipients like before although they were administered according to the company's rules.

4. Camondos' loss of interest in their legacy in Istanbul

A few months after the contract was signed following Abraham's death in December 1889, Moïse and his cousin Isaac took the lead of the family business. Neither of the two was really interested in the financial and real estate business; moreover, as their ties with Istanbul were not as deep and emotional as their predecessors' ones, they decided to close the bank's Istanbul office 1894,[50] and their real estate company, headed by Léon Piperno, remained limited to the administration of their fortune. Some of their property was sold just after the death of Abraham between 1890 and 1899: the house on Mertebani Street, 5, property in Beykoz, Çamlıca,[51] a brick factory in Sütlüce, plots in Duvarcı and Kömürcü streets in Pera, in Feriköy, Lüleci Hendek, Bulgaria and the prestigious *yalı* in Yeniköy were altogether sold for 143.920, 59 French francs.[52]

A letter from Piperno to Moïse de Camondo in 1902 revealed one of the problems regarding real estate ownership in the context of companies. Although the affair was not mentioned in detail, we understand that during the liquidation of the bank, the State wanted to claim back the property, registered in the company's name, and was ready to pay 40,000 liras for it. Piperno tried to avoid this by using the Grand Vizier Said Pasha's position.[53] In 1908, Moïse de Camondo paid a visit to his motherland with his 16-year-old son Nissim de Camondo to initiate him into the real-estate of his family, just as Moïse had been in his young age.

We learn from Şeni's work that there is no information on Nissim's impressions and reminiscences from this journey; in fact it seems that

---

[50] Şeni & Le Tarnec, *Les Camondo ...*, p. 150–154. Tugay & Tugay, *Kamondo Han*, p. 136.

[51] The mansion with its vineyard was sold to Necib Molla. Tugay & Tugay, *Kamondo Han*, p. 110.

[52] *Ibidem*, p. 128.

[53] *Ibidem*, p. 143.

neither Nissim, nor his son-in-law Léon Reinach, were ever really interested in the family business.[54] Thus, after the death of Nissim during the Great War, in 1917, Moïse de Camondo decided to liquidate his business. In his letter to the Imperial Ottoman Bank, dated January 23, 1919, he declared that Isaac de Camondo & Cie had entered into liquidation,[55] and two months later, gave orders to Piperno to liquidate the business, and particularly the remaining real estate in Istanbul (Fig. 13).[56]

5. As a conclusion: Taksim residential buildings project

The Camondos, with some hundred property in their hands, were certainly the major investors in real estate of their time. Thanks to Abraham Salomon's insight and leverage, the Camondos were able to use to their advantage the winds of change of the third quarter of the 19th century. His major investments were in Galata, a district which rapidly gained importance and value during his lifetime. Here, he participated in a variety of infrastructural projects which would increase the value of the region and consequently his own assets and profits. Thus, property meant business for Abraham Salomon, who could circumvent the ban on property ownership for foreigners thanks to his influence at the Porte.

54 Şeni & Le Tarnec, *Les Camondo …*, p. 211, 253.

55 OBA, OFTC0052, Camondo & Cie., November 21, 1903.

56 AMNC, Letter of Moïse de Camondo to Piperno, April 4, 1919 reproduced in Şeni & Le Tarnec, *Les Camondo …*, p. 250.

Tab. 2. Summary of Camondo's property[a]

	Apartments	Han	Shops	Land	Others	Na	Total
Pera	8	0	1	2	0	1	12
Pera-Galata	2	0	4	1	0	2	9
Galata	25	12	9	2	0	4	52
Stamboul	0	1	0	1	0	0	2
Others	8	0	1	10	7	3	29
Total	43	13	15	16	7	10	104

Sources: BOA, EV 20150, "Mösyö Kamonto'nun malı olan 23 kalem mahaller ile vakıflarının isimleri ile senedlerin mikdâr ve kayıdları," 1283.Ş.23–1283.Za.13 (December 31, 1866–March 19, 1867).
AMNC, "Recensement des titres de propriété opéré le 8 Avril 1884."
AMNC, "Notes of Tedeschi on the properties of Camondos," 1888.
AMNC, Contract related to the foundation of the real estates company, Constantinople, July 1, 1899. *Annuaire Oriental*, 1881, 1895, 1899, 1909, 1914.
Nora Şeni, "The Camondos and their imprint on 19th century Istanbul," *International Journal of Middle East Studies*, 1994, volume 26, p. 663–675.
[a] See the detailed list in Tanatar Baruh, "The transformation of the "modern" axis of the nineteenth-century Istanbul" ... Appendix BB. Camondo property: List, plans and photos, p. 405–422.

The area from Perşembe Pazarı to the bridge was already the most prestigious and central area of Galata, which soon turned out to be exclusively dedicated to commercial activity.[57] Camondo, when investing in Galata, found that the district was already promising in terms of investment, and the new office *hans* that he constructed offered the facilities requested by the companies of the time. The decline in high

[57] A file in the Ottoman State Archives on the request for permission to construct shops in place of Muslim houses destroyed by fire gives us some clues on the transformation of the area in the 1850s. Although in the beginning the original owners wanted to reconstruct their houses, they changed their mind. It was said that the reason behind such a request was the increasing demands of Christians to settle in the district, and because of the proximity of the plots to the mosque, it was preferable to transform the houses into shops. As such it would be ensured that non-Muslims would only be there during the day and not in the night. The Sultan accorded his permission under the condition that houses would not be constructed on it. BOA, İ.MVL 361–15961, "Galata'da Perşembe Pazarı'nda yanan İslâm hâneleri arsâlarına mağaza yapılmak üzere ruhsat verilmesi," 1273.Ca.13 (January 9, 1857).

rents as more and more new buildings were constructed[58] indicates a corresponding decrease in the returns from investments in commercial buildings in the 1890s. By then, the majority of real estate investments had moved towards apartment buildings mostly situated in the upper parts Galata, which would in turn decrease in importance as apartment buildings expanded towards the more prestigious Pera.

The fact that the Camondos left the city in 1867 could be considered as one of the reasons why they did not seem to develop a greater interest for investment in the northern part of Pera that was rebuilt after the 1870 fire. Moreover, although the initial investments seemed more or less consistent in terms of their location, the great variety of property located in different districts of the city acquired by the family at a later date gives the impression that an increasing portion of their property was acquired against outstanding debts. When the family business was transferred to the fourth generation who, contrary to their forefathers, did not have any real emotional tie with the city, the Camondos tried to rationalize the administration of their property by selling the real estate they did not want to invest in, only keeping the core property which would be liquidated in 1919.

Nevertheless, Isaac de Camondo was appointed as the vice-president of the Paris-based National Company for Trade, Industry and Agriculture in the Ottoman Empire[59]: Initially it aimed at conducting activities in trade, industry, urban and rural property, and to establish a company which would last for fifty years and would give credits on mortgage. However, it was soon decided that it would deal exclusively with property; it therefore founded the Ottoman Real Estate Credit Company in 1914[60] to build residential buildings in Taksim (Fig. 14). One would be

58 See the case of Saint-Pierre Han or that of Camondo Han in Yorgancılar. A note in the Tedeschi notebook informs us that both stages of the *han* rented to Société générale at 1,000 liras per year would decrease to 300 liras, if they left. When the Imperial Ottoman Bank left Saint-Pierre Han, the owner was unable to rent the offices for the same amount (450–500 liras instead of 1,350). See: MNC, Notes of Tedeschi …, p. 3 and SALT Research, Saint Peter Church Archive, SPC 030-0731, "Lettres de la Municipalité du 6e Cercle réclamant les taxes échues de Saint-Pierre," September 26, 1896–December 10, 1896.

59 "Le Champ de Mars et la Caserne du Taxim," *La Gazette financière*, 1911, no. 68, p. 8. Jacques Thobie, *Intérêts et impérialisme français dans l'Empire ottoman (1895–1914)*, Paris, Publications de la Sorbonne, 1977, p. 470.

60 The other founding partners were Banque de Paris et des Pays-Bas, Société générale, the Imperial Ottoman Bank, and Banque de Salonique whereas the Ottoman

tempted to think that their interest in real estate investment in Istanbul was still quite alive, even if it has come to mean business rather than prestige, the latter being transferred to the Parisian life of the family's last generations.

On the eve of World War I, the Camondos were among the aforementioned private investors who disappeared from Istanbul's urban scene, leaving behind their property that would later be transferred to the third parties. The construction of buildings in place of military barracks and drill ground of Taksim were also not realized (Fig. 15). The uncertainty brought by the war, along with the difficulties in sourcing construction material, the soaring inflation, and the shortage of labour all led to the project's failure,[61] and the construction of the area, with the exception of the barracks would only be possible through different means in the 1930s (Fig. 16).[62]

---

government kept the privilege of subscribing for 100.000 liras. "Société immobilière de Constantinople," *La Gazette financière*, 1914, no. 238, p. 287.

61 Ali Akyıldız, *Osmanlı Dönemi tahvil ve hisse senetleri. Ottoman securities*, Istanbul, TEB, 2001, p. 244.

62 Pervitich draws first the Talimhane area, the drill ground and its surroundings, in his plan number 12 and dated 1925. In this plan the plots are shown but buildings do not appear yet. The construction of the area is drawn later on a plan dated 1943 under the same number. Nur Akın states that these apartment buildings in art deco style were constructed by the renowned architects of the time such as Vedat Tek, Seyfi Arkan and Sedad Hakkı Eldem. Nur Akın, "Talimhane Yayalaştırma Projesi'nin Düşündürdükleri," *Arredamento Mimarlık*, January 2005, no. 176, p. 84. For the Ottoman Real Estate Company and its investment projects in Istanbul, see Lorans Tanatar Baruh, "İstanbul Emlâk Şirket-i Osmaniyesi'nin Yatırımları: Karaköy Borsa Hanı, Taksim Kışlası ve Talimhane," *Toplumsal Tarih*, April 2013, no. 232, p. 30–35.

Fig. 1. Camondo Han in Karaköy Square, 2008. Photo: İzzet Baruh.

Fig. 2. Postcard showing Karaköy Square and the last floor of Camondo Han at the back of Commission Han, posted in 1919. Editor: Max Fruchtermann. SALT Research, Photographs & Postcards Archive.

Fig. 3. Latif Han in Perçemli Street, 2008. Photo: İzzet Baruh.

Fig. 4. Yakut Han in Billur Street. Detail of the Entrance, 2008. Photo: İzzet Baruh.

Fig. 5. Saatçi Han in Perşembe Pazarı Street, 2008. Photo: İzzet Baruh.

Fig. 6. Camondos' Property in the Vicinity of the Galata Bridge. Charles E. Goad Insurance Map, Vol II: Péra & Galata, no. 28, 1905. Institut français d'études anatoliennes Map Collection.

Fig. 7. Camondo Lüleci Han in Mahmud Paşa Yokuşu, 2008. Photo: İzzet Baruh.

Fig. 8. Camondo's Residences in Galata . Charles E. Goad Insurance Map, Vol II: Péra & Galata, no. 27, 1905. Institut français d'études anatoliennes Map Collection.

Fig. 9. Camondo's apartment building in Felek Street, 2008. Photo: İzzet Baruh.

Fig. 10. Camondo's apartment building reconstructed, in Yazıcı Street, 2008 ; Photo: İzzet Baruh.

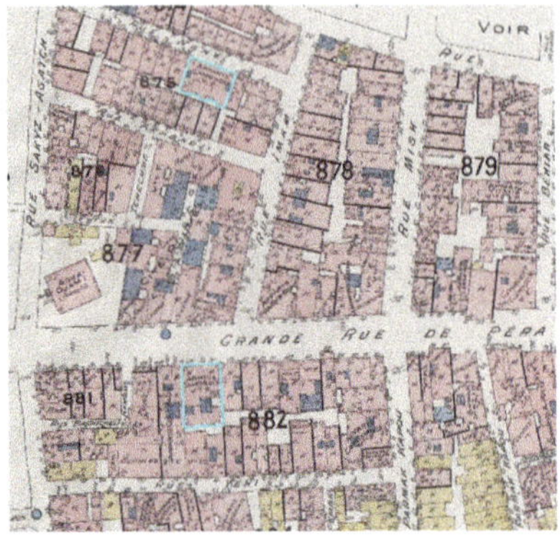

Fig. 11. Camondo's Property in Pera. Charles E. Goad. Insurance Map, Vol II: Péra & Galata, no. 40, 1905. Institut Français d'Etudes Anatoliennes Map Collection.

Fig. 12. Camondo's Apartment in Pera,Beyoğlu Municipality, 2004. SALT Research, Photographs & Postcards Archive.

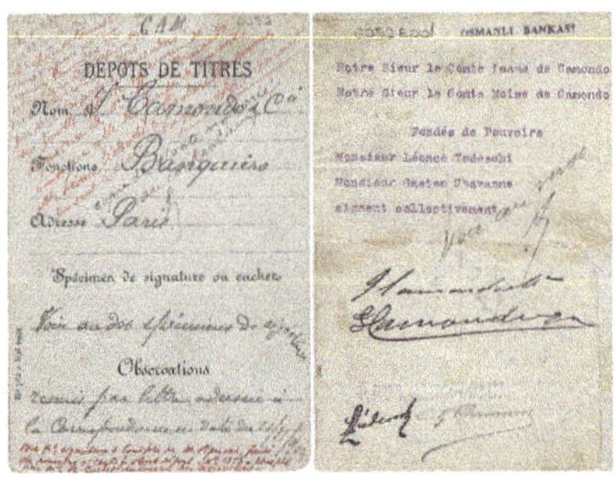

Fig. 13. Imperial Ottoman Bank Customer Stocks & Bonds Deposit Card of I. Camondo & Cie, SALT Research, Ottoman Bank Archive.

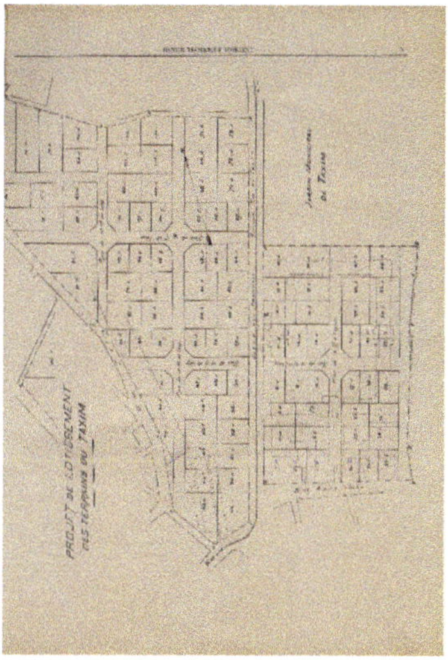

Fig. 14. Drawing of the apartment buildings projected for the Taksim barracks and Talimhane ; *Revue technique d'Orient*, no: 7, March 15, 1911, p. 5.

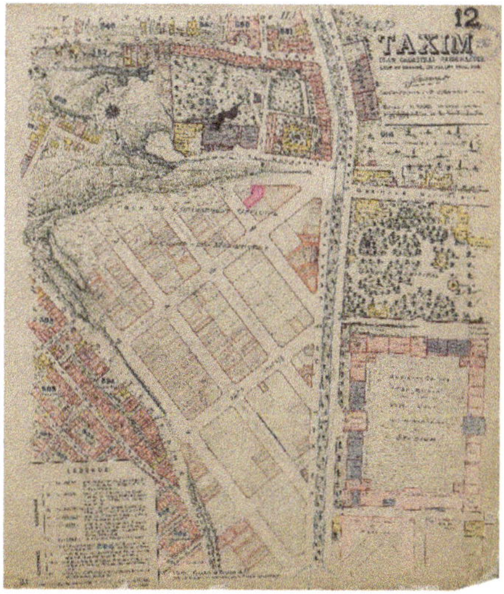

Fig. 15. Map of Taksim showing the official plots drawn for apartment buildings in Talimhane Jacques Pervititch Insurance Map, no. 12, 1925. Institut français d'études anatoliennes Map Collection.

Fig. 16. Aeral photo of Taksim showing the new apartments in the Talimhane area and Taksim barracks, 1930s. SALT Research, Ali Saim Ülgen Archive.

Chapter 2

The "new bank" and the culture of the *Haute Banque* in France in the second half of the 19th century

Nicolas Stoskopf

In an article published sixty years ago, David Landes challenged the idea of a conflict in 19th century France between the old and new banks; that is, between the *Haute Banque* on the one hand, and public limited banks (also called joint-stock banks or credit institutions) on the other.[1] Arguing that this is a common preconception based on the rivalry between the Rothschild and Pereire families, he emphasized the diversity of activities carried out by the "old bank" and its capacity for adaptation, put the novelty of this "new bank" into perspective and demonstrated that the former largely participated in the creation of the latter. He conceded, however, that this banking revolution provided opportunities to new entrepreneurs and that the old bank was not uniformly favourable to new methods. He concluded by affirming that events were more complex than the traditional narrative indicates and that the relationships between people and institutions were more nuanced than has previously been supposed.

Following in the footsteps of Landes, one is now tempted to say that things are in reality even more complex than he presented them: indeed, his argument was based on the Rothschild-Pereire rivalry and the merchant bank as represented by the Crédit mobilier model; and he neglected other players and other types of joint-stock banks with specialized functions, such as mortgage banks and deposit banks. If we take this diversity into account and look at the broader picture, we can identify a

---

1 David S. Landes, "Vieille banque et banque nouvelle: la révolution financière du XIXe siècle," *Revue d'histoire moderne et contemporaine*, 1956, tome III, p. 204–222.

paradox: on the one hand, we can observe the limits of the *Haute Banque*'s influence on the creation of the new bank: entire swathes of the latter escaped the former's grasp and, if there are remarkable examples of collaboration and osmosis, the two banking circles remained quite distinct in terms of their socio-cultural character. But on the other hand, the uses, methods, and culture of the *Haute Banque* influenced the new bank to the point of changing the trajectory of many establishments. In short, the players changed, but the same traditions were passed down. If this mixture of genres seemed to work for a certain period, it most often led to financial disasters and major crashes in the 1880–1890s.

To carry out this study, we must start from the foundation of Comptoir national d'escompte de Paris in 1848 (the special case of the Banque de France, founded in 1800, which was in fact a new bank co-managed by the *Haute Banque*, will not be addressed here[2]), and trace the developments through the 1890s – in short, an overview of half a century.[3]

1. The limits of the *Haute Banque*'s participation in the creation of the new banking economy

It is important to distinguish the two processes of founding public limited banks, with or without the *Haute Banque.*

A. The Crédit mobilier (1852), a longstanding exception

The Crédit mobilier, created in November 1852, was initially the tree that hid the desert (and not the forest). It was an exception from the

---

2 Alain Plessis, *Histoire de la Banque de France*, Paris, Albin Michel, 1998. *La Banque de France et ses deux cents actionnaires sous le Second Empire*, Geneva, Droz, 1982. *Régents et gouverneurs de la Banque de France sous le Second Empire*, Geneva, Droz, 1985.

3 We will draw in particular on previous personal studies: Nicolas Stoskopf, *Banquiers et financiers parisiens*, series. *Les patrons du Second Empire*, tome 7, Paris-Le Mans, Picard-Cenomane, 2002. Nicolas Stoskopf, "What is the Parisian *Haute Banque* in the 19th Century," Journée d'études sur l'histoire de la Haute Banque, Paris, 2000; https://halshs.archives-ouvertes.fr/hal-00441164. Nicolas Stoskopf, "From the private bank to the joint-stock bank: The case of France (second half of the 19th Century)," in *Companies-Owners-Employees*, Proceedings from the 6th Annual Congress of the European Business History Association (EBHA), August 22–24, 2002, University of Helsinki, Department of Social Science History, 2003 [https://halshs.archives-ouvertes.fr/hal-00934946].

outset, marked by the influence of the *Haute Banque* on the new bank. The initiative came from Benoît Fould of the Fould & Fould-Oppenheim banking house, who subscribed 35 % of the capital along with his allies Oppenheim, Heine and Ratisbonne, and became chairman of the new company. They brought with them a few other heavyweights from the Parisian *Haute Banque* who joined the board of directors: Charles Mallet, Ernest André, Achille Seillière,[4] and Adolphe d'Eichthal. Alongside them, the Pereire brothers, Émile and Isaac, emerged as newcomers, not being bankers in the strict sense of the word: they contributed 28.6 % of the capital, and Isaac took over as vice-chairman while Émile Pereire kept his distance in order to devote himself to the Compagnie des chemins de fer du Midi (the Southern railway).

This balance was disrupted when Benoît Fould's attacks of insanity forced him to resign and hand over the chairmanship to Isaac Pereire in December 1853. From that point on, the Crédit mobilier came fully under the leadership of the Pereire brothers who could count on the loyalty of their allies from the *Haute Banque*: the Foulds, the Mallets, the Seillières, the D'Eichthals, etc. The Crédit mobilier is therefore a remarkable example of the *Haute Banque*'s participation in the new bank – so much so, in fact, that the *Haute Banque* should have been able to determine its direction. And yet, circumstances decided differently.

B. Where the Haute Banque was conspicuously absent

However, the *Haute Banque* was not a stakeholder in many other new banking projects: First, the Comptoir national d'escompte de Paris was created on the initiative of the Republican government in March 1848.[5] But if the Rothschild and Fould banks contributed to its share capital, it was only along symbolic sums (40,000 and 30,000 francs out of a total of 20 million francs, a third of which was paid by private shareholders), and their representatives did not join the board of directors.

---

4 See: Nicolas Stoskopf, "Les Seillière, une grande famille ?," in Jean-Michel Boehler, Christine Lebeau & Bernard Vogler (eds.), *Les élites régionales (XVIIe-XXe siècles). Construction de soi-même et service de l'autre*, Strasbourg, Presses universitaires de Strasbourg, 2002, p. 161–170. Raymond Dartevelle (ed.), *La banque Seillière-Demachy. Une dynastie familiale au centre du négoce, de la finance et des arts, 1798–1998*, Paris, Perrin-Fondation pour l'histoire de la Haute Banque, 1999.

5 Nicolas Stoskopf, "La fondation du Comptoir national d'escompte de Paris, banque révolutionnaire (1848)," *Histoire, Économie et Société*, 2002, no. 3, p. 395–411.

The Crédit foncier de France was gradually created in February and December 1852.[6] Those who subscribed capital included the Pereire brothers and their friend Adolphe d'Eichthal, who had made a name for himself in the *Haute Banque* of the July Monarchy, but went bankrupt in March 1848 and reinvested at the end of 1849 on a smaller scale. He was among the directors, known as a 'friend of the Pereires' as much as a representative of the *Haute Banque*.

The *Haute Banque* did not play a role in the introduction of the English deposit bank model in France either. The initiative was taken by two businessmen close to Comte de Morny, Armand Donon and William Gladstone, who submitted their project at the end of 1855.[7] This sparked the immediate reaction of James de Rothschild, who in January 1856 brought together other heads of the *Haute Banque* houses (Cahen d'Anvers, Davillier, Hentsch, Mirabaud, Vernes) and railway financiers (Bartholony, Dassier, Talabot) in what was known as the *Réunion financière*.[8]

This group is traditionally presented by historiography as being an anti-Pereire syndicate: there is certainly truth to this, but the chronology and the circumstances suggest that it was formed first and foremost to counter the Donon-Gladstone project. Moreover, the *Réunion financière* submitted its own competing project in turn. The government and the Council of State rejected the two projects, and James de Rothschild did not insist then: he remained completely removed from the banking revolution and continued to use the "old methods" which had been very successful for him up to that point.

Donon and Gladstone did not let the matter rest there and, in March 1857, approached the members of the *Réunion financière* to propose merging the two competing projects, but they were bitterly dismissed by their

---

6 Aline Raimbault and Henri Heugas-Darraspen, *Crédit foncier de France, itinéraire d'une institution*, Paris, Éditions du Regard, 1994.

7 Guy Beaujouan and Edmond Lebée, "La fondation du Crédit industriel et commercial," *Histoire des entreprises*, November 1960, p. 5–40. Nicolas Stoskopf, *150 ans du CIC (1859–2009), une audace bien tempérée*, Paris, La Branche, 2009 (published online under the title: *Histoire du Crédit industriel et commercial (1859–2009)*) [https://halshs.archives-ouvertes.fr/hal-00946846].

8 About the *Réunion financière*, Bertrand Gille, *La Banque en France au* XIXe *siècle*, Geneva, Droz, 1970. Alain Plessis, *La politique de la Banque de France de 1851 à 1870*, Geneva, Droz, 1985. Bertrand Gille published the "Procès-verbaux de la Réunion financière (1856–1860)," *Histoire des entreprises*, May 1962, no. 9.

interlocutors, who did not want to compromise their vision "with names that had not yet earned their stripes (that is, their grades or credentials) in what we call the *Haute Banque* and *Haute Finance*.[9] Incidentally, we learn here what the *Haute Banque* truly was: not a group that can be defined by objective criteria (seniority, financial strength, international reach, etc.), but a club of private bankers who co-opted members by sorting those with whom they could work from those with whom they didn't want to work. It was founded on the reputation of its members, who refused to mix with outsiders. Indeed, not one Parisian *Haute Banque* house subscribed even a share of Crédit industriel et commercial (CIC), the first French deposit and commercial bank established in Paris in May 1859; none of its representatives chose to associate themselves with this project that perfectly illustrates banking renewal.[10]

The *Haute Banque* was active neither in the Société de dépôts et de comptes courants – also founded by Armand Donon in July 1863, on the same day as the Crédit lyonnais, but with three times the capital – nor in the regional deposit banks established in the following months in Marseille, Lyon and Lille.[11]

Until the beginning of the 1860s, the *Haute Banque* abstained as a rule from the creation of the new banks. At this point, it missed the train and remained on the platform. It seems therefore finally that Landes was wrong … But further case studies might anyway somehow confirm his opinion.

C. The emergence of truly "mixed" projects

The *Haute Banque* would not show any interest in the "new bank" again until the foundation of the Crédit lyonnais in July 1863: bankers from Geneva (Hentsch, Paccard), joined by others (Mirabaud, Bischoffsheim, Vernes, Blount), subscribed for shares, and the first two joined the board of directors.[12]

---

[9] *Journal du Crédit public*, March 7, 1857, cited by G. Beaujouan and E. Lebée, *op. cit.*, p. 12.

[10] Memorandum of association, April 30, 1859, study by Pascal Dufour, Paris (National Archives, MC XLVIII).

[11] Nicolas Stoskopf, *150 ans du CIC*, *op. cit*, p. 60–66.

[12] Jean Bouvier, *Le Crédit lyonnais de 1863 à 1882: les années de formation d'une banque de dépôts*, Paris, SEVPEN, 1961.

Then in May 1864, the foundation of Société générale was accompanied by an even more widespread adhesion of the *Haute Banque.*[13] The point of departure was the alliance formed between a man of the new bank, Alphonse Pinard, sub-director of the Comptoir d'escompte de Paris, with two *Haute Banque* heavyweights: Louis Bischoffsheim, who belonged to a network of powerful European families including the Goldschmidts, the Bambergers, the Cahen d'Anvers, the Erlangers, the Sterns and the Hirschs; and Édouard Hentsch, who represented the Protestant bank of Geneva. This alliance was forged at the beginning of the 1860s at the Crédit foncier colonial, an establishment supported by the Comptoir d'escompte and located at 14, rue Bergère.[14]

This trio took part in the foundation of the Banque de crédit et de dépôt des Pays-Bas in February 1863 in Amsterdam, and especially in that of the Société générale in May 1864 in Paris, of which Hentsch and Pinard, along with Talabot, were appointed the first directors. The project incorporated many *Haute Banque* houses (Blount, Cahen d'Anvers, Davillier, Mirabaud, Perier, etc.). James de Rothschild, however, once again kept his distance: "Why change when we're doing well?" he said in October 1865.[15]

If we can speak of a true dynamic with regard to the Pinard-Bischoffsheim-Hentsch group, it is that its creative productivity did not stop there and even survived the death of Pinard in October 1871. Bischoffsheim and Hentsch joined forces again to set up the Société générale algérienne in October 1866, the Banque franco-égyptienne in March 1870, and most notably the Banque de Paris et des Pays-Bas in January 1872, with a significant investment from Alphonse Pinard's widow. As for Édouard Hentsch, chairman of the Comptoir d'escompte since November 1873, he was also among the primary founders of the Banque de l'Indochine in January 1875.[16]

---

13 Hubert Bonin, *Histoire de la Société générale.* Tome I. *1864–1890. Naissance d'une banque*, Geneva, Droz, 2006.

14 Nicolas Stoskopf, "Alphonse Pinard et la révolution bancaire du Second Empire," *Histoire, Économie et Société*, 1998, no. 2, p. 299–317.

15 Study into the principles and general facts governing fiduciary and monetary circulation *(Enquête sur les principes et les faits généraux qui régissent la circulation monétaire et fiduciaire). Dépositions écrites françaises et étrangères* [1865], Paris, tome 1, 1867.

16 Marc Meuleau, *Des pionniers en Extrême-Orient. Histoire de la Banque de l'Indochine, 1875–1975*, Paris, Fayard, 1990.

There is no need to look further down the timeline, as these last examples clearly demonstrate that aside from the Rothschild exception, there was no longer any opposition between the "old" and "new" banks. And yet, osmosis was still far from being achieved.

D. Two socio-cultural models

Each of these banking categories had its own type of banker who belonged to a distinct world. The *Haute Banque* was cosmopolitan and multi-faith, with well-known contingents: a group of German Jewish bankers, a Swiss Protestant group, and a third French group comprising Catholics (Laffitte, Seillière, Perier), Protestants (André, Mallet, Neuflize), and Jews (Fould).[17] It was, however, homogenous from a sociological point of view: these bankers belonged to families who had long been engaged in business trading, or even in banking, and often represented the second, third, or even later generations in banking.

The new managers offered another profile altogether: they came from similar cultural backgrounds, as they were all French and Catholic (except the Pereires with regard to religion), but their social backgrounds differed, from the trade workers' milieu (Pinard) to the aristocracy (D'Audiffret, De Germiny). Their professional experience was also varied: many came from careers in civil service (D'Audiffret, Frémy, Soubeyran) or the legal professions (Donon, Henri Germain). Those who could draw on a familial business background and the cultural transmission that went along with it were in the minority.

And so this rapid historical tour leads to a nuanced assessment: aside from the case of Crédit mobilier, it would take some time to see the "species barrier" crossed, without completely erasing the socio-cultural differences between the two banking worlds. The least we can say is that the *Haute Banque* long remained circumspect and selected its investments with careful rigour. It nevertheless showed an interest in the merchant bank (Crédit mobilier, Crédit lyonnais, Société générale[18]) while

---

17 The Foulds, originally from Fulda, were present in Lorraine since the end of the 17th century. The Mallets, Huguenots who emigrated from Rouen to Geneva, returned to settle in France in 1713.

18 Before they became more rigorous in the use of their resources and moved towards the deposit bank model starting in the 1880s, Crédit lyonnais and Société générale

remaining disinterested in other types of banks (discount, mortgage and deposit banks).

2. The new banking system influenced by the culture of the *Haute Banque*

But did the new managers behave so differently from their *Haute Banque* peers? Were they not finally led to recycle old practices and to "ape" the methods of the *Haute Banque*? We can point to three symptoms of this influence, three behavioural trends (especially in establishments created without the participation of the *Haute Banque*!), mainly seen in the 1860–1890s: personalization; confusion between private and public interests; and abuse of articles of association. In a certain number of cases, this led to a final catastrophe and personal ruin.

A. Personalization of management

Even certain contemporaries were shocked by the personalization of banking management, which is in opposition to the status of a public limited company. Thus, the economist Alfred Neymarck said in 1880: "In France we have a very fine group of first rank credit institutions, [which are] huge associations, vast aggregates of interest; according to the law and their articles of association, they are limited companies. Well, well! In reality, they are as far from 'limited' as possible. What one sees in them, and sometimes above them, is the name of a talented founder, an experienced administrator, a competent and approved director, a noted and well-known organizer."[19]

Stable management was probably a significant factor in this identification, even in certain semi-public establishments whose directors were appointed by the government: 20-year mandates were commonplace and often ended only after the appointee's death. Henri Germain held the record, having remained at the head of Crédit lyonnais for 42 years until his death (1863–1905).

---

acted like mixed banks, as has been clearly demonstrated by Jean Bouvier and Hubert Bonin, respectively.

19 Quoted by Claudio Jannet, *Le capital, la spéculation and finance au XIXe siècle*, 1880, p. 177.

This identification worked for the press and the public in much the same way as it did for the *Haute Banque*. For example, the government's nomination in 1859 of Marquis d'Audiffret – a 71-year-old eminent specialist in public finance and veteran of the Cour des comptes – as chairman of the CIC, a private limited company, was intended to reassure the public in the face of the presumed dangers of an anonymous deposit bank. He brought his name, his reputation, and a life in service of the public interest, as well as a consistent record of rigorous management and the caution of an irreproachable senior official. This service background must have acted as a guarantee, much like the personal fortunes of the *Haute Banque* patrons did.

But the negative consequence was the risk that managers would feel untouchable and irremovable.

B. The risk of confusion of interests

From here to regarding the company as personal property was a step that some individuals appeared to take. At any rate, there was clearly confusion between private and public interests. The Comptoir d'escompte de Paris and the Crédit foncier de France offered good exemples thereabout.

If the Crédit foncier colonial was supported by the Comptoir d'escompte de Paris, which allowed the bank to use its premises and staff, it was not based on statutory links – investing in limited companies was prohibited at the Comptoir d'escompte – but rather on the personal investments of its directors: Alphonse Pinard, its sub-director, subscribed 4.7 % of its capital and became its first chairman. When Société générale was founded, he subscribed 16,000 shares for the Comptoir and 7,450 for his own account (a capital investment of 3,725,000 francs).

When it came to foreign loan investments, which the Comptoir specialized in from 1864 onwards, Pinard "gambled" recklessly with the company's money and with his own. Rumour had it that the Comptoir had 15 million francs' worth of its director's discounted bills in its portfolio! Pinard was brutally attacked – by shareholders at general meetings, in lampoons and in the press. He was accused of betraying the Comptoir's original mission, of scarcifying money in France, of using the company for his own personal ends, and of getting rich at the shareholders' expense and on the backs of the investors who subscribed to the

Comptoir's "rotten" loans.[20] But he could take refuge behind the excellent results of his establishment, which paid out a dividend in excess of 10 % from 1864 to 1868.

At the Crédit foncier, the Governor and Sub-governor, Louis Frémy and Georges de Soubeyran, did not draw a very clear line between their public function and their private affairs either: Frémy chaired a number of companies whose activities would generate conflicts of interest with the Crédit foncier. When the governors were in difficulty following the Egyptian bankruptcy of April 1876, Soubeyran behaved like a major banking house patron: he placed a governors' guarantee of sixteen million francs on the table, fifteen million of which he provided himself (and which he would never recover).

When his appointment was revoked in August 1878, he explained several times why he had acted in this manner: he believed that bankers, even in limited liability companies, should put their personal fortune on the line in order to inspire confidence in their partners and their clients, and that their wealth is, in the end, the strongest proof of their competence. It was the reasoning of an 'old bank' patron.

C. Abuse of articles of association

What threatened shareholders and institutional creditors in all their forms (in particular depositors) was non-compliance with articles of association, which could sometimes be totally misused. Even in the establishments that were, in principle, the most closely monitored, this type of practice was common: at the CIC, despite the protests of observers, reserves were used for operations strictly prohibited by the articles of association (article 5), because another article, no. 59, gave the Board the responsibility to "determine its use"![21]

If the Saint-Simonian project, carried mainly by the Pereires and focused on the functional specialization of credit institutions, advanced for a time on the heels of the interventionism of the Bonapartist State, the liberal turning point of 1860 was the heyday of banking confusion. The apparent specialization of the major credit establishments diminished,

---

[20] Journal *Comic-Finance*, April 21, 1870. H. Mathorel, *La situation de nos sociétés de crédit: le Comptoir d'escompte*, Paris, 1873.

[21] Nicolas Stoskopf, *150 ans du CIC*, *op. cit.*, p. 65–66.

either by changes in the articles of associations, or by the creation of subsidiaries with more liberal articles. Thus, in July 1860, Frémy founded the first institution of Crédit agricole and ensured that its articles of association would authorize him to operate in ways that were prohibited at Crédit foncier. His resources were partly diverted through his Marseilles branch to unsecured short-term investments in Turkey, Russia, and Tunisia and above all in Egypt.

As the chairman, in a private capacity, of the Société générale algérienne, a company which could compete with Crédit foncier, Frémy also distanced himself from his obligations under the treaty signed with the State in May 1865. Instead of financing public works in Algeria, he steered the company towards more directly and rapidly profitable operations such as the territorial liberation loans of 1872–1873, advances to the Spanish Treasury and the Spanish Mortgage Bank and other foreign loans. At the beginning of the Third Republic, it was common knowledge that the *Hôtel d'Évreux*, the residence of the Governor of Crédit foncier, on the *place Vendôme*, was the place where all major business was shared out among Parisian bankers.[22]

This case illustrates a marked trend in the French banking system, i.e. the progressive slide of specialist establishments towards mixed banking, the all-purpose bank which was undifferentiated and modelled upon the private bank. This new model combined traditional banking operations (exchange, discount, recoveries), financial operations (issuing loans or company shares), international trade and direct investment (railways, mines, heavy industry, real estate).

We can observe similar behaviour from the deposit banks (Crédit lyonnais, Société générale), even when this was not their original intention. Donon, for example, championed the notion, in France, of the distribution of banking tasks and a deposit bank along English lines, in which the assets were as liquid as their liabilities, concentrating solely on short-term credit.[23] Yet he strayed from his own beliefs when he created a multifunctional business group made up of separate companies, but nonetheless interconnected on a human level by the same group of

---

22 Jean Bouvier, "Les intérêts financiers et la question d'Égypte (1875–1876)," in *Histoire économique et histoire sociale*, Geneva, Droz, 1968, p. 241–269. Jean-Pierre Alline, *Banquiers et bâtisseurs, un siècle de Crédit foncier, 1852–1940*, Toulouse, CNRS, 1983.

23 He defended these positions at the *Enquête sur les principes …, op. cit.*

shareholders and directors, and financially by cross-holdings or cross-debt.

The new managers certainly used new tools – those of the public limited company and the expansion of resource collection – but finally aligned themselves to the behaviour of traditional bankers, competing with them on their own territory and sharing the best sources of profit with them. In this way, the contribution of the new bank finally proved more quantitative than qualitative as it provided a new boost to French capitalism, particularly during the Second Empire.[24]

D. Sanctions against bad practices

This worked for a while. However, the euphoria was short-lived and the aftermath was like the painful hangover which follows one drink too many. From 1873, the Great Depression provided the necessary toxic agent, and the effect was maximized when Republican politicians settled a few accounts with bankers who were regarded as creatures from the Second Empire.

The majority of these new managers were sanctioned one after another, by the government or by the market: the dismissal of Frémy and Soubeyran in 1877 and 1878, Guillaume Denière's resignation from the chairmanship of Société générale in 1886, the bankruptcy of Comptoir d'escompte in 1889, now chaired by a defector of the *Haute Banque*, Édouard Hentsch, who allowed his establishment to be dragged into a disastrous speculation in copper, and the bankruptcy of the Donon and Soubeyran business groups in 1891 and 1894, respectively. The only establishments that made it through the period relatively unharmed were those that had not strayed too far from their articles of association (CIC) or that returned to a stricter deposit banking practice in time (Crédit lyonnais, Société générale).

What was sanctioned, in fact, was not the new bank, but the behaviour of these neo-bankers, who lacked a strong banking culture or tradition in their family and seemed fascinated by the behaviours and methods of the "old bank." They acted as if they owned the capital and took a great many liberties with their shareholders and the articles of

---

[24] As demonstrated by Rondo Cameron, *France and the Economic Development of Europe, 1800–1914*, Princeton, Princeton University Press, 1961.

association, which they were supposed to respect. While the economic and political environment remained favourable, they met with success, but the spectre of failure darkened the horizon at the end of the 1870s. Only a few managed to escape the disaster: either those who were already dead, or those who had been more far-sighted and prudent in turning their situation around, such as Germain at Crédit lyonnais.

3. Conclusion

The "new bank" owed little to the *Haute Banque*: it was carried by new men, new resources and new ideas. In the end, the human and financial contributions of the *Haute Banque* were relatively marginal, except in the clearly identified merchant banks such as the Crédit mobilier or, twenty years later, the Banque de Paris et des Pays-Bas. The paradox is that the new bank struggled to shake off the cultural and behavioural heritage of the *Haute Banque*: it adopted the latter's practices and customs – for the best, as long as the financial and economic profits and successes allowed it to conceal its dark side, to some extent – but finally for the worst when the economic and political environment took a different turn. It seems legitimate, then, to wonder if the *Haute Banque* did not hand down the worst of itself and leave the new bank a rotten heritage.

Chapter 3

The *Haute Banque*, American Civil War debt, and the integration of 19th century capital markets

David K. Thomson

Historians have for decades described in detail the power of the *Haute Banque* – a loaded term that is easily definable yet at the same time laden with complexities. Nevertheless, *Haute Banque* institutions became a fundamental element of 19th century French banking. One definition of the *Haute Banque* describes it as a group of individual enterprises or companies of persons distinguished by their honour, respectability, financial power, and activities oriented towards international money markets. Despite these identifiable traits, a conservative investment approach was the norm for the *Haute Banque* in the 19th century.

But these fundamental ideals of the *Haute Banque* extended beyond the Parisian capital, and not just in reference to their focus on international markets. In the wake of the 1848 revolutions that swept Europe, many other continental bankers outside France reassessed their relationships with other firms on the continent and newly expanding markets like the United States. In doing so, such banks expanded the notion of the *Haute Banque* beyond the French borders and revealed the power and pull of relationship banking in an era where sales increasingly could be viewed in transactional banking quantities more in line with the 20th century.

1. European *Haute Banque* and the US market

Perhaps this is best illustrated by the rise in stature and capital of banks in the German states. Financial centres in Frankfurt, Hamburg, and Berlin grew in the 1860s and 1870s to previously unforeseen levels.

Chief in the rise of these financial centres was American debt – specifically American federal debt tied to the American Civil War. By 1869, $1 billion of the federal debt could be found in foreign hands, meaning nearly half of the US debt could be found abroad. Yet while the quantity of debt held overseas should offer a moment of reflection, it was in fact the interpersonal arrangements within Europe and across the Atlantic based on *Haute Banque* principles that offer a window into late 19th century financial markets and changing investment strategies for the *Haute Banque*.

These debt transactions of the 1860s and 1870s belie a larger point, however, as the relationship banking practices endemic to the *Haute Banque* began to grapple with overall volumes of bond sales that came to define the transactional banking of the 20th century. True – this was a far cry from volumes of the latter half of the 20th century as commoditized finance took hold over Wall Street and global markets – yet it opens a unique window into how relationship banking attempted to grapple with this issue.

The French *Haute Banque* of the 19th century – and specifically the Jewish and Protestant banks – had focused on international markets since their rise to power in the first half of the 19th century. Houses like Rothschild, Mallet, Hottinguer, Hentsch, and Mirabaud all migrated in some form to Paris in the 19th century, but maintained ties to their foreign homes through general travel, marriage, and business travel that helped to facilitate contacts in the forms of agents. All these acts helped to reinforce the cosmopolitan motif of these financial institutions and also aligned them with international banking interests in the 19th century. While many proclaim that the height of the *Haute Banque* could be located from 1840 to 1860, the reality is that for certain houses, the 1860s and 1870s offered a wealth of opportunity and central to that was American debt and the partnerships facilitated through formal syndicates and more informal arrangements predicated on familial and religious networks. Such acts not only on the continent but across the Atlantic played an instrumental role in the emergence and success of certain French houses and the new wave of French banks founded in the 1870s that were partially underwritten by the *Haute Banque*.[1]

---

[1] Many of these ideas are addressed in further detail in Alain Plessis, "The Parisian '*Haute Banque*' and the international economy in the nineteenth and early

In June 1853, foreign countries held approximately $53 million in American railroad securities and $27 million in U.S. government bonds. Largely owned by German, French, Swiss, and British investors this represented a modest investment by foreigners in American securities – both state debt and railways. By 1869, government bonds held by foreigners had spiralled upwards to $1 billion and railroad securities had grown to approximately $250 million. What accounted for such a stark transformation? On one level, the expansion of railways in the United States and their subsequent capitalization undoubtedly played a role. But this does not account for the exponential growth as it pertained to U.S. securities. In order to understand this, one must look at the rapid financial transformation afforded by Union securities during the American Civil War and in its immediate aftermath.[2]

Despite the successful efforts to sell bonds domestically among the northern populace, international sales were important and indeed necessary for the triumph of the Union cause. Union bond sales on an international level quickly became a necessity in order to stabilize domestic markets. In essence international sales acted as a validation for all future success of Union securities – the mere act of European investment had an undeniable impact amongst financiers in the North who shared their confidence with the general public. All told, several hundred million dollars worth of these bonds made their way across the Atlantic during the war itself and found investors in Britain, France, Belgium, Ireland, Russia, Switzerland, Austria, Italy, the German States, and the Netherlands.

Although Britain served as the perceived primary market for sales, in reality the underappreciated continental sales in the Netherlands and especially amongst the anti-slavery population of the German states constituted the true market for international sales – revealing the political and economic pull of the continent and a reflection of the larger integration and sophistication of global capital markets by the middle of the 19th century.[3]

---

twentieth centuries," in Youssef Cassis and Philip Cottrell (eds.), *The World of Private Banking*, Farnham, England, Routledge, 2009, p. 127–140.

2 Mira Wilkins, *The History of Foreign Investment in the United States to 1914*, Cambridge, Harvard University Press, 1989, p. 76–80, 116, 118. Only six American railroads at this time had foreign ownership that exceeded 10 %.

3 Studying international bond sales during the American Civil War does not come without difficulty. Whereas the ledgers associated with the Bureau of Public Debt housed at the National Archives carry meticulous records of domestic primary

In fact, the sale of Union securities during the war and its immediate aftermath perhaps belied a starker transformation: that the national financial infrastructure created during the war through the Legal Tender Act and National Banking Act took a national moment and portended an international revolution for American banks. What had previously existed on local levels was now elevated to a national financial structure that took on transnational ramifications. Furthermore, the war and international markets for Union securities on such a large level took antebellum British structures and flipped them on their head. Antebellum British banking partnerships with American partners (not sending agents as British banks were accustomed to doing) became a model that American banks took as they expanded into international markets.

No longer subservient to British banks, the post-war period witnessed American finance wading into international markets like never before, and fundamental to this were Union bonds. Not only that, but the relationships developed between American banks and European partners – as well as major European banks and their partners demonstrated the widespread nature of *Haute Banque* ideals by the second half of the 19th century. Indeed, relationship banking was fundamental to understanding global financial networks.[4]

Nineteenth century financial markets – and specifically the vibrant bond markets – are vital to understanding the political economy of this era. Bond issues and the market response to them reflected the political and diplomatic stakes of the time period. Established European houses such as the Rothschilds, Barings, and Hope & Co. (along with their correspondent banks) played as crucial roles in politics as foreign ministers at times. Thus by the time of the American Civil War, the Lincoln Administration knew that an American bond issue that reached European markets played a crucial role in the fate of the Union abroad.

---

purchases, secondary market sales (including to European banks) become much more difficult to trace. Additionally, many European firms' records have been lost to wars and time. Furthermore, Wall Street financial firms acting on behalf of international clients could hold bonds, so that the physical bonds never travelled overseas.

4 Such a notion of British bank inversion is addressed by Jay Sexton in his recent work, "International finance in the Civil War Era," in Jorg Nagler, Don Doyle, and Marcus Graser (eds.), *The Transnational Significance of the American Civil War*, Basingstoke, Palgrave Macmillan, 2016.

The debate over international sales, however, began at home. While some criticized foreign sales and emphasized the political advantage of a purely domestic issue in wartime, others in Washington recognized the power of international support and foreign "buy in" to the Union cause. Secretary of the Treasury Salmon Chase remarked that a foreign loan helped to ensure "all hopes and all fears that the existing rebellion will result in a dismemberment of the American Republic are alike groundless." Indeed, the passage of the initial loan bill included a provision for $50 million of the bill in a direct European loan. The Secretary vacillated extensively on the issue, however, during the course of his tenure and by the summer of 1864 seemed content to go in for a foreign loan, even though in doing so, he told newspaper editor Horace Greely, "galls me."

Chase's successor, William Pitt Fessenden, demonstrated initial interest in pursuing an international direct loan, but by the fall of 1864, his opinion on the matter had soured, even leading him to declare in December 1864, "This nation has been able, thus far, to conduct a domestic war of unparalleled magnitude and cost without appealing for aid to any foreign people." While Fessenden's claim is certainly one of dubious validity, it was undoubtedly the case that at the highest levels of government the messaging on international bond sales (direct or indirect) was muddled at best.[5] In March 1865, one Pennsylvania newspaper boldly proclaimed: "We have not been compelled to go abroad in search of a dollar of the one that has been laid out on our army and navy. No American agent has had to bend before the capitalists of Amsterdam and Frankfort and London, asking for money on their own terms. The wealth of America has proved equal to the part which our money has performed in the maintenance of the national integrity." While such claims instilled great pride in the Northern populace in the waning months of the war, the reality was certainly different.[6]

---

5 Salmon Chase to William Aspinwall, March 30, 1863, Salmon Chase Papers, Historical Society of Pennsylvania (HSP), Philadelphia, Pennsylvania; Salmon Chase to Horace Greely quoted in Jay Sexton, *Debtor Diplomacy: Finance and American Foreign Relations in the Civil War Era, 1837–1873*, New York, Oxford University Press, 2005, p. 128. William Pitt Fessenden quote, in Sexton, *Debtor Diplomacy*, p. 129.

6 *Columbia Spy*, March 4, 1865.

Civil War general and New York City Democratic Party politico Daniel Sickles also advocated for a foreign loan, but emphasized the power of a widely held bond issue abroad. Writing from New Orleans, Sickles exclaimed "our bonds should be placed within the reach *of our friends in Europe* by a *popular* arrangement that will enable the *producing class* to buy them *in small amounts* – by means of pamphlets, friendly journals, and advertisements, the inducement of a fair commission held and to judicious agents – the excellence of the security and ample return in the way of interest would be made apparent to our friends and to all who like a proposition + safe investment … The same could be done in Germany and probably in France." Little did Sickles and others know that the United States government and financial houses abroad were already undertaking such activity.[7]

William Evans, an English financier, sold a small portion of bonds ($30,000) abroad at the behest of British politician John Bright. For Jay Cooke, such an endeavour was an exception and a reflection on Cooke's seeming desire to keep the bonds on this side of the Atlantic at virtually all costs. That said, Evans continued to make sales on behalf of Cooke and his firm. In September 1864, following the prompt sale of $100,000 worth of 5–20s, Evans wrote to Cooke to speak of the prospect of further European sales. "Demand on the continent for your gov't securities is wonderful," exclaimed Evans; more tellingly he ended the letter by telling Cooke, "perhaps, they [the U.S. government] will follow your advice and avail themselves of the offers of the German bankers."[8]

That said, for the most part, Cooke really did restrict his focus domestically, despite any rhetoric otherwise – a stark contrast to his post-war securities career when he hawked bonds in Europe – contributing significantly to the global financial crisis of 1873. Once the benefits and interest in foreign sales were apparent, the Cookes and many others began to heartily endorse such an approach, at least in theory. Writing in August 1864 from Paris following travels in Germany, Henry Cooke (head of Jay Cooke & Co.'s Washington house) wrote to his brother noting that a massive opportunity for foreign investment had been missed. "There was never a finer opportunity," lamented Henry, "for safe operations on

7 Daniel Sickles to Salmon Chase, July 5, 1864, Chase Papers, HSP; Domestic bond "czar" Jay Cooke made an overture for foreign sales in late 1863.

8 William Evans to Jay Cooke, September 7, 1864, Jay Cooke Papers, HSP.

a large or small scale with good margins in gold paid in advance." Henry went on to say that offers were made to him for purchases of 5–20 bonds in excess of $20 million dollars, but he had only committed to $100,000 in sales up to this point (via the British banking house Barings) and awaited further consultation with his brother upon his imminent return to the states. By 1865, Jay Cooke had been sold on the power of international sales: "If we go into the agency matter," he wrote Henry, "we must at once lay on plans to cover the whole world. France + California included." But by the time he completed his transformation, other banking houses – largely headquartered abroad with American partners – were already doing a brisk business in overseas bonds.[9]

As far as American financiers and politicians were concerned, Britain served at the outset of hostilities as the market of greatest importance from both financial and diplomatic perspectives. "English sympathy is very apt to follow English Capital. This is one good political reason for placing bonds in Europe," financier William Aspinwall remarked. Union officials were well aware of the fact that any hope of international support on behalf of the Union – or the Confederacy for that matter – would be heavily tied to the financial interests of the City of London.

Any efforts on the part of Parliament at Westminster would be linked closely to the actions a few miles away to the east in the City of London proper and relied upon several key actors who were members of Parliament as well as a part of the financial elite. The likes of Rothschild, Barings, and a host of other financial institutions emanating out from the Bank of England on Threadneedle Street would be the financial fuel for Union success. Once more, the actions of Britain would have a powerful impact upon their European neighbours of France and Napoléon III's subsequent approach to the matter at hand.[10]

---

9 Henry David Cooke to Jay Cooke, August 19, 1864, Jay Cooke papers, HSP; Jay Cooke to Henry David Cooke and Harris Fahnstock Jan 24, 1865, Jay Cooke Papers, HSP.

10 William Aspinwall to Salmon Chase, March 21, 1863, Chase Papers, Library of Congress (LC), Washington D.C.

2. German markets involved overseas

Despite the allure of the London and Paris financial markets, the primacy of Union sales abroad during the war centred around the German states. In the German states, Frankfurt emerged as a financial capital of the mid-19th century and became especially important as the American sovereign debt market of greatest importance. In the wake of the 1848 Revolutions that swept Europe, Frankfurt became for many Americans the political and economic capital of the German states. For many Americans, Frankfurt symbolized liberalism and democracy. Such an atmosphere cultivated in this period served to foster extensive ties between the North and the region when the time of the Civil War emerged.

In addition, connections between the regions centred around extensive migration from the German states to the northern part of the United States, but especially emanating from Frankfurt and the surrounding region of southern Germany. Between 1850 and 1860, approximately 1.1 million immigrants arrived from the German states in America. Of those 1.1 million, approximately 25 % emigrated from Frankfurt and its surrounding environs. As historian Patrick Gaul astutely points out, the city of Frankfurt also became a point of interest for Americans travelling abroad and by 1864, 222 Americans called Frankfurt home.[11]

By 1863, such actions paid tremendous dividends as U.S. Consul William Murphy reported to Secretary of State William Seward that the demand for bonds was "so extensive as generally to exceed the supplies in the market." Such interest in Germany accelerated following the Union victories at Gettysburg and Vicksburg in July 1863. "The transactions in U.S. bonds," Murphy reported that summer, "assumed, in fact, an astonishing extent." The activity in Europe more broadly spiked beginning in the fall of 1863, largely owing to the rumour that a large German bank would float a loan to the federal government – something that would create a snowball effect of further financial support for the North. On October 3, 1863, Murphy wrote to Secretary Seward regarding the 10 million sterling (slightly under $50 million) 6 % loan that was potentially going to be offered by the Bank for Commerce and Industry in nearby Darmstadt.

---

11 Patrick Gaul, *Solidarität auf Kredit: Verflechtungen zwischen Mitteleuropa und Nordamerika vor dem Hintergrund des amerikanischen Bürgerkrieges*, PhD Thesis, Frankfurt Goethe University, 2018, p. 145–47.

The bank was of "good reputation and credit" as far as Murphy had uncovered and had the potential to open the floodgates for European loans to the American government – causing some excitement on European exchanges. The efforts in Germany were fairly widespread – even Karl Marx purportedly purchased bonds in 1864. In addition, the efforts on the part of the French bank Erlanger to finance a cotton loan on the part of the Confederacy can be seen in a somewhat different light when one realizes that Erlanger purchased Union bonds at the exact same time on the Frankfurt *Börse*.[12]

Germany could even lay claim to have the resident with the single largest investment in Union bonds. According to his obituary, George William Whistler, half-brother of famed American artist James Whistler, was allegedly the largest investor in Union securities during the war from his retirement home in Frankfurt. The capital stemmed from Whistler's work in Russian railroads. Despite this claim, the above obituary could not be located at the Library of Congress within the Pennell-Whistler papers, and consultation with the most recent authority on the Whistler family, Daniel Sutherland, confirmed that there is no evidence to support the notion that G. W. Whistler actively supported the Union cause, and in fact, the family was far more sympathetic to the Confederacy.[13]

Alexander D. White, future co-founder and inaugural president of Cornell University, commented on the success of Murphy and Union securities during his travels through Germany in 1863. "William Walton Murphy of Michigan," remarked White, "had labored hard to induce the Frankfurt bankers to take our government bonds, and to recommend them to their customers, and had at last been successful." Upon his departure from Germany in late July 1863, White recalls one of his last experiences in Germany being a stroll with Murphy to the *Zeil* – a busy Frankfurt thoroughfare not far from the *Börse* (and currently the home

---

[12] August Belmont to Salmon Chase, August 15, 1861, August Belmont Papers, Library of Congress, Washington D.C. For more on Murphy and Pike see, Sexton, *Debtor Diplomacy*, p. 21–25; William Murphy to William Seward, July 27, 1863, RG 59, NARA II; Murphy to Seward, October 3, 1863, RG 59,NARA II. Niall Ferguson, *The Cash Nexus: Money and Power in the Modern World, 1700–2000*, London, Basic Books, 2001, p. 5–6; Murphy to Seward, January 20, 1863, RG 59, NARA II.

[13] Obituary, Pennell-Whistler Papers, Library of Congress.

to American fast-food restaurants and European chain retail stores) and encountering the Vice Consul who handed Murphy a newspaper. Murphy "tore it open, read a few lines, and then instantly jumped out into the middle of the street, waved his hat and began to shout. The public in general thought him mad … but as soon as he could get his breath, he pointed out the headlines of the newspaper. They indicated the victories of Gettysburg and Vicksburg …"[14]

The bonds issues were floated in Frankfurt and absorbed by some of the larger houses such as Karl Pollitz, M.A. Gruenebaum & Ballin, Lazard Speyer-Ellissen, Metzler, and Seligman & Stettheimer to name but a few of the banks – many of whom had developed partnerships with American based firms. Murphy used the press to his advantage. Publications such as the *Neue Frankfurter Zeitung* and *L'Europe* championed Union bonds sales while simultaneously downplaying efforts for a Confederate bond floated by Erlanger. The end result was the claim that "hundreds of millions" of dollars were invested in American securities on the Frankfurt exchanges alone – a claim that seems on the surface to be quite credible.[15]

Various American government officials in the German states outside of Frankfurt also relayed the interest of the German people in American bonds as the calendar turned to 1864. Vice-Consul W. Marsh of Hamburg wrote to Secretary of State Seward in July 1864, to communicate that "I had a call from Mr. Hoffsteadt, The object of his visit was to

---

14 Quoted in Margaret Sterne, "From Jonesville," p. 256–257. Alexander White famously noted in his autobiography of an instance while in London where he tried to exchange greenbacks for sterling and was sternly rebuked by the cashier. "Don't offer us any of those things; we don't take them; they will never be good for anything," White, *Autobiography*, 1: 94.

15 Udo Heyn, *Private Banking, op. cit.*, p. 274–275. Korach, *Das Deutsche Privatbankgeschaeft*, 31. Handelskammer Frankfurt (ed.), *Geschichte der Handelskammer*, p. 1141–1142. The newspapers are also enlightening in other regards. For instance, a September 1, 1864, ad in the *Neue Frankfurter Zeitung* contains in very large font the word "*verloren*" ("lost") regarding $10,000 in 5–20 bonds bound for Amsterdam on the Steamer Scotia from New York City for the account of a Phillip Abraham Cohen in Frankfurt. The ad appears several times in September 1864 before disappearing. It is worth noting that the $1,000 bonds contained within this group of $1,000 and $500 bonds were initially purchased by Jay Cooke & Co. in May 1863, as part of a batch of $2 million $1,000 bonds. For more on Austrian security depreciation see Platt, *Foreign Finance*, p. 90, 92–96 and Wood, *Economic Rise*, p. 145.

inform me that he had had a consultation with eminent bankers on the subject of a Premium Loan of one thousand million dollars, as a preliminary step in support of his offer to the United States Government." Marsh similarly relayed the impact of Lincoln's successful reelection of Abraham Lincoln in the fall of 1864 and that proposals of international loans had tremendous impacts on international sales. "At any rate, I can truly say that the German Loan which I was the promoter of had the effect here of selling millions of our bonds," remarked Marsh. He similarly relayed the faith of German financiers when he remarked in the spring of 1865, just a month before Appomattox that one group declared: "Only we hear of Richmond falling you will see your stocks advance to 75 per cent of their value in Hamburg Change."[16]

But perhaps one of the biggest contributing factors to the success of Union bonds in the German states stemmed from the personal and professional partnerships of banks in the United States and in Frankfurt – an essential component of relationship banking in the 19th century. Indeed, the majority of these bonds surely made their way overseas via New York City houses that had German connections. One prime example is that of J. and W. Seligman Co. Joseph Seligman originally immigrated from Germany to the United States in 1837 and quickly built a dry goods empire. By the time of the war, Seligman's company produced a large quantity of uniforms for the Union Army. That being said, Seligman recognized the potential to become a significant player in international finance.

As such, Joseph sent his brother Henry to Frankfurt in 1862 in the hopes of establishing a German house and Joseph subsequently followed him across the Atlantic spending a significant amount of time in the region during the war. Joseph became active in the securities market during his visit. Seligman conveyed his confidence in American securities early on. "Now I confess," admitted Seligman, "that altho' I know the U.S. to possess unparalleled resources, I sometimes doubt whether any people in any nation can successfully go on for years adding 1000s of millions to their National debt. If such a nation however does exist, there is no doubt but that the U.S. are that nation." While the exact total of Seligman sales remains a mystery owing to the likely destruction

16 W. Marsh to Seward, July 30, 1864, RG 59, NARA II; W. Marsh to Seward, RG 59, NARA II, November 23, 1864; Marsh to Seward, December 5, 1864, RG 59, NARA II; W. Marsh to Seward, March 8, 1865, RG 59, NARA II.

of pertinent materials by an archivist some fifty years ago, the firm undoubtedly played a critical role in financing Union broads in the German states.

The exact quantity of sales on the part of the Seligmans is a source of great debate. In 1931, journalist Linton Wells completed his institutional biography *The House of Seligman*, in which he claimed that the firm sold $200 million in securities during the war in Germany. Others have subsequently used this number as well. While Wells appeared to reference material that contained specific numbers, regrettably the Civil War era material related to the Seligman businesses has largely been lost and rumoured to have been thrown away by an archivist in the subsequent decades following the completion of Wells' work. The only materials that continue to remain are a couple of letter-books (business and personal) that only reach to April 1864. Based on these books, however, it would seem to question the figure $200 million. Delores Greenberg's work has also questioned this figure owing to the fact that so many of the bonds were purchased by the conglomerate of Jay Cooke & Co and his subcontracting agencies. That being said, in essence both sides could theoretically be correct as Cooke could have enacted the primary sales with Seligman far more active on the secondary market. Regrettably we may never know owing to evidentiary limitations.[17]

3. The rush of European investors: Transatlantic bridgeheads within *Haute Banque*

By the summer of 1865, with the war for all intents and purposes over, European investors, most notably the Dutch and Germans, pushed foreign investment in the United States well beyond its pre-Civil War levels. Word quickly spread across the United States of the insatiable demand for federal debt in the German states. Just months after the war had ended, the *New York Times* republished a letter that had originally run in the (then) Hamburg, Germany suburb of Altona. "It is highly gratifying to observe here," the letter began, "a daily increase in the price and popularity of our stocks. While all other securities are depreciating,

[17] For more on Greenberg's questioning of the Seligman figure, see Delores Greenberg, "Yankee financiers and the establishment of Trans-Atlantic partnerships: A re-examination," *Business History*, 1974, volume 16, no. 1, p. 17–35.

only United States stocks seem to gain ground. The largest amount of business done in these securities hitherto was last week – one person having bought the enormous amount of five hundred thousand dollars for himself, besides being a permanent holder to the amount of two hundred thousand dollars." The letter went on to conclude, "The Germans are a thrifty and safe calculating people, ever choosing the safest and best marks for their products, whether money or goods, and they seem to be now the war is over, perfectly satisfied to deposit their savings in American securities."[18]

But perhaps a letter from an American living in Frankfurt in 1868 really got to the heart of the matter perhaps more so than any other letters transmitted to the United States Treasury Department. "Really this market controls the European," the letter began, "Here all the great sales are made, and to this point are all the stocks sent from New York, and here the coupons on nearly all the stocks held in Europe are sent for sale and collection. Frankfurt is about the only city which has its branch houses in the United States." The letter went on further to note the plethora of German incorporated banks with capital requirements based largely in American securities. Specifically, the American financier referenced the Banks of Meiningen and Darmstadt, who among other banks "hold several millions of our Five-Twenties."[19]

European periodicals also supported these assessments. In November 1868, a report from a Belgian financial paper made its way into the *Atlanta Constitution* of all American newspapers. The report from the *Écho de Bourse* proclaimed: "The Germans have a most complete knowledge of the resources of the United States. They have placed a great deal of money in the American bonds … The daily sales which are made at Frankfurt, Hamburg, Bern, and Berlin can be almost compared with the sales and transactions of Wall Street."[20]

But what accounted for interest in the German states that fed the demand? For some, the bonds were purchased in anticipation of European conflict between the French and German states. One report from Germany indicated, "a real investment demand for 5–20s is now setting in from the peasantry and that class of people, especially since the

18 "Five-Twenties Abroad," *New York Times*, April 2, 1867.

19 "American Securities in Germany," *New York Times*, April 26, 1868.

20 "American Securities," *Atlanta Constitution*, November 28, 1868.

war looks inevitable."[21] For others, bonds took on geopolitical relevance. "These bonds also invite a large immigration," one article proclaimed. "When the people of Europe receive that the great republic meets its interest promptly, and that too of so high a rate … the emigrant carries with him his bonds, because he feels the confidence that he can realize upon them … It seems to us that the missionary influence of those bonds in Americanizing Europe, in drawing its people to our government, and in making them as it were the constant watchers of American progress, is indeed boundless."[22]

Another letter written from an American in Germany reinforced this sentiment of the power of bonds on immigration. "These bonds are the most powerful and influential emissaries you could have sent over to the Old Continent to convert the masses in republican principles. They never before heard so much talk about America; your means and resources, your future and your prospects, are discussed everywhere, and in such favourable terms that emigration is the leading topic among the sturdy masses; and the next year will bring you for every $1,000 of your bonds taken in Germany, at least one of her sturdy sons."[23]

Whatever the reason for the demand in these bonds (a topic to fully explore another day), the German banks that facilitated these widespread sales relied on a variety of networks and aggressive investment strategies (despite the seemingly "safe" nature of bond investments.) First and foremost, these networks were predicated on familial social networks, in another word, kin. A pipeline emerged between New York and Frankfurt specifically, in which American houses bought extensively on behalf of their German relatives and then sold them across the Atlantic. Indeed, the majority of these bonds surely made their way overseas via New York City houses that had German connections. One prime example is that of J. and W. Seligman Co.

Seligman recognized the potential to become a significant player in international finance. As such, Joseph Seligman sent his brother Henry to Frankfurt in 1862 in the hopes of establishing a German house, and Joseph subsequently followed him across the Atlantic spending a significant amount of time in the region during the war. While the firm did

---

21 "American Bonds Hoarded Abroad," *Gettysburg Sentinel*, June 26, 1866.

22 "Our Bonds Abroad-A Powerful American Missionary," *Semi-Weekly Wisconsin* (Milwaukee), February 28, 1866.

23 *Ibidem.*

not formally establish a banking house in Frankfurt until 1864, Joseph became active in the securities market during his visit.

By the spring of 1867 (the earliest point in the post-war period with surviving records), Seligman & Co. was sending more than $100,000 in bonds daily overseas. Perhaps most interestingly, Seligman distinguished in his letters between "small 5/20" orders – that is, those that were bonds of $50 or $100 and other 5/20 orders that were bonds in larger denominations. In fact, as spring turned to summer in 1867, Seligman's correspondence revealed a decided pattern. For London, the orders were almost always for larger sized bonds with less of an emphasis on the $50 and $100 bonds. On July 19, 1867, Seligman wrote to the London house to note that $300,000 worth of 5/20s had been purchased – $50,000 of which were small 5/20s.

The note continued remarking that the London house was still owed another $500,000 in large 5/20s as well as $40,000 of small 5/20s and $58,000 in '81s (i.e. bonds maturing in 1881). Conversely, Joseph Seligman wrote daily to the Frankfurt House relaying orders that by early August were exclusively for small 5/20s in varying amounts that at times surpassed $100,000 daily. The small sized bonds making their way to Frankfurt would seem to reiterate the claims of American representatives abroad who emphasized the fact that the issues were wildly taken up in Frankfurt by investors of all classes.[24]

Another example of familial ties involved Speyer Ellisen. New York City based Speyer & Co. represented the interests of their partner institution L. Speyer Ellisen – a bank with decades of ties to Frankfurt. Speyer & Co. purchased heavily for the Frankfurt house accounts which then proceeded to sell their bonds far and wide in the German states. Much like Seligman – the familial ties of the Speyers enabled a healthy exchange of securities across the Atlantic to meet the growing demands of the German populace and their neighbouring countries. While the exact sales on the part of the Speyers have been lost to time, surviving correspondence for the firm and their rivals reveals an intense interest and pursuit of American bonds.

Bethmann Bank in Frankfurt likewise played a substantial role in the post-war period and reveals another networking approach – one based on faith. For the Bethmanns represented the single largest Christian bank in

---

24 Seligman Co. Papers, Bass Library, Oklahoma University, Norman, Oklahoma.

Frankfurt – an outlier in a city largely dominated by Jewish bankers. In the aftermath of the war through the end of 1865, the firm purchased slightly over $350,000 worth of 5–20s. Investments rebounded in the first quarter of 1866 to the tune of $163,000 followed by $122,500 in the second quarter. A third quarter of $104,000 followed by a fourth quarter that brought in $227,000 demonstrated a continued interest on the part of the firm and their European clients in United States bonds.

In 1867, Bethmann upped their investment in American 5–20s to $1,354,100 with additional purchases of 81s and 5–20s from 1865 (combined total of some $71,100.) In 1868, the stakes grew even higher with $2,134,900 in 5–20s purchased by the Frankfurt house and half a million dollars worth of additional Civil War bonds. The first two quarters of 1869 (the current end of records held by this author) totaled some $782,700 in 5–20 Civil War bonds. In the post-war period, the firm's investments went to a wide range of clients – although only some records have survived.

Of these records, were a wide variety of banks in Frankfurt as well as established citizens. But Bethmann's clients went far beyond Frankfurt itself – and even nearby suburbs of the town such as Wiesbaden – to Hamburg, Berlin, Munich, Leipzig, and smaller locales such as Aachen, Heidelberg, Marktheidenfeld, Wildenberg, Freiberg, Freidburg, and Meisbich. But the clients also spread to France, Austria, Switzerland, Ukraine, Italy, Russia, Greece, and Romania. All of these examples ranged from established financial institutions like the Norddeutsche Bank of Hamburg (an early house to join Deutsche Bank) and Marcuard & Co of Bern, Switzerland. Some individuals included the Greek ambassador to Austria who came to run the Austrian National Bank as well as lesser known individuals whose records have been lost to history such as a "Frau Von Owen" of Frankfurt as well as Georg Kerua of the same city. The source of bonds for the firm stems from a wide variety of Christian New York City houses – many of which had ties to Jay Cooke & Co – the domestic agent for bond sales during the American Civil War.[25]

But transatlantic ties only represented one dimension of the *Haute Banque* dynamic, for German ties to the French *Haute Banque* proper came to entail an even larger percentage of the market. One of the most preeminent firms that comprised the French *Haute Banque*, Rothschild

---

[25] Bethmann Bank Collection, Institut für Stadtgeschicte, Frankfurt, Germany.

& Frères of Paris, offers one of the best examples of these exchanges. Part and parcel of this exchange was the Rothschild agent in the United States, August Belmont. Born in 1813 in the Rhenish village of Alzey, by the age of fifteen Belmont found himself under the watchful eyes of family friends – the Rothschilds – who apprenticed him to their Frankfurt branch. Belmont ultimately found his way to the United States in the midst of the Panic of 1837 and it was in this light that he came to work on behalf of all Rothschild accounts, chiefly though, London and Paris. But if Belmont is a factor in this story – it's only because of the head of the Paris house, James de Rothschild, enabled him to participate in the exchange (but in a limited fashion.) J. de Rothschild ran the Paris branch until his death in 1868 and it was the Paris branch that proved most important in the American bond market.[26]

In fact, it was the partner institutions throughout Germany that proved instrumental in purchases for the Paris house. While these purchases initially were for arbitrage purposes, it evolved over time into widespread purchases for clients. L. Behrens & Söhne in Hamburg, Bleichröder Bank in Berlin, and Warburg Bank in Hamburg all worked heavily in their respective markets for Rothschild Frères. And this was just on behalf of the Rothschilds, to say nothing of their own investments on their own accounts – be it clients or personal accounts.

For the Bleichröder house, the active market in Berlin proved remarkably fruitful. By the summer of 1865, the firm was making daily purchase for the Paris house of Rothschild in the neighbourhood of close to $100,000 on average. Additionally, the house also made purchases for clients either on behalf of the Rothschilds, or their own clients who currently found themselves in Paris – such as Victor Renary. By the latter part of 1866, the Bleichröders were making significant purchases on behalf of the Rothschilds, including a $700,000 purchase in 5/20s in November and $480,000 of the same issue on Valentines Day 1867. Surviving records indicate that these purchases largely went to clients – and were not held on personal accounts.[27]

---

26 Katz, *August Belmont*, 3–6. For the most comprehensive analysis of N.M. Rothschild & Sons, see Niall Ferguson, *The World's Banker: The History of the House of Rothschild* (London: Weidenfeld & Nicolson, 1998.)

27 July 8, 1865, July 22, 1865, July 24, 1865, August 23, 1866, November 23, 1866, and February 14, 1867, Bleichröder to James de Rothschild, Bleichröder Bank Correspondence, Rothschild Co. Papers, *Archives nationales du monde du travail*, Roubaix, France.

For the Hamburg houses of Warburg and Behrens, it was much more of the same. For Behrens in particular, the daily purchases averaging some $50,000 became a regular occurrence by 1866 for House Rothschild. Likewise, the Rothschild house based in Frankfurt and run by Mayer Rothschild also coordinated with the Paris house. By 1869 the Frankfurt house made daily purchases (alternating between House purchases and those for individual clients) numbering in the range of $50,000. Thus, for the Rothschilds, the post-war period presented a wonderful opportunity to invest heavily in American bonds.[28]

The Rothschild reliance on their German partners reflected a significantly greater interest in American bonds purchased through Jewish connections within Europe. On top of that, these purchases found themselves predicated on familial and religious ties across the Atlantic. All of this is to say that while the traditional French *Haute Banque* had been known to expand into continental Europe in the mid 19th century, this interest in American securities – specifically here in the case of the Rothschilds – marked a new investment opportunity and pattern. Working in arrangements that epitomized *Haute Banque* ideals, the Rothschilds coordinated closely with German banks in Berlin, Hamburg, and Frankfurt to access American bonds on favourable terms. Access to these funds increasingly came not from the American agent for the Rothschilds – August Belmont – but through their *Haute Banque* contacts in the German states, long after the arbitrage market for these bonds had effectively dried up with the reintroduction of the transatlantic cable. Indeed, when these bonds sold above New York values in the German states and elsewhere, the Rothschilds still opted for the European transactions, revealing the ties that bind for these banking families.

Furthermore, the refinancing of American debt in 1871 and 1873 offers another window into the Rothschilds. While the houses in London, Paris, and Frankfurt were divided on how heavily to invest in the first refinanced American loans of 1871, they all significantly invested in the 1873 loan and even became members of a large financial syndicate to

---

28 January 18, 1866, April 13, 1866, April 20, 1866, and August 10, 1866 Behrens Co. to James de Rothschild, Behrens Co. Correspondence, Rothschild Co. Papers, *Archives nationales du monde du travail*, Roubaix, France; May 12, 1869, May 18, 1869, August 30, 1869, and October 28, 1869, Mayer Rothschild to James de Rothschild, Frankfurt House Correspondence, Rothschild Co. Papers, *Archives nationales du monde du travail*, Roubaix, France.

sell the bonds in Europe and even further afield. The London house in particular expanded relationship banking during this period with some of their sales. Lombard Odier (Geneva), Oppenheim & Cie (Cologne), Avigdor l'aîné & fils (Nice), Banque d'Alsace-Lorraine, and the Enskilda Bank (Stockholm) all represented investors in American debt at this time – perhaps for the first time – and conducted these transactions in large quantities more akin to 20th century transaction banking standards. Bleichröder Bank's purchase of $5 million in American debt in 1873 on a single day perhaps is one of the most profound examples of these high volume transactions that were becoming the norm by the 1870s. On top of these types of transactions, the Rothschilds sold bonds to various institutions in emerging markets that were founded/ underwritten by *Haute Banque* houses of the "old" financial world.

The Banque de Constantinople purchased $560,000 in these 5 % bonds as part of their initial capitalization and was comprised of British, French, and local Galatian bankers that underwrote it. The Moscow Discount Bank's $50,000 purchase to base their capitalization is even more intriguing when one realizes the bank was founded by two of the leading German firms in Moscow – L. Knoop and Wogau & Co. Other efforts at capitalization by Société générale and Bank of Australasia also reveal these relationship bankers breaking into new markets – foreshadowing the evolving financial landscape by the turn of the century on a global stage.

4. Conclusion: The *Haute Banque* apprenticeship of transatlantic finance

Writing many years after the Civil War, the established Frankfurt banker Saemy Japhet wrote of his introduction at a young age to American securities: "There was hardly an investor in South Germany who did not buy United States bonds … They all believed in the ultimate victory of those who identified themselves with the cause of liberty … The profits made in American securities and American trade were one of the stepping stones on which the newly enriched world of Germany could tread."[29]

29 Quoted in Stanley Chapman, *The Rise of Merchant Banking*, London, George Allen & Unwin, 1984, p. 46.

Japhet's commentary is illuminating and places a distinct emphasis on American bonds as a fundamental building block for the German economy. But this point is parcel of something even deeper – that is the fundamental arrangements that facilitated these sales. Familial and religious connections across the Atlantic for many German banks helped to expand the German market while informal partnerships also took advantage of the American bond market. Yet, much of this was predicated on honour and trust – particularly for informal arrangements that came into being during this period of rapid financiarization.

Despite the perception of government bonds as safe investments, an ocean separated these houses from the United States government. This was a nation comprised of a collection of states, many of whom had defaulted on state bond issues in the antebellum and immediate post-war period. It was imperative for these German banks to have close connections via partnerships stateside. It was these German banks that projected *Haute Banque* ideals (and *Haute Banque* connections) across the Atlantic, opting to push beyond the fairly conservative notions of "international markets" put forward by their French rivals (or in some cases partners).

It was this bold step forward on the part of German banks that slowly roped in the *Haute Banque parisienne* to this wider financial market. The prestige and reputation of the *Haute Banque* when coupled with the more aggressive investment pursuits of German banks fostered new relationships that open a window into deeper international financial markets centred around an emerging German financial sector.

Part II

From history to present times: Issues of path dependency

Chapter 4

BNP Paribas and the legacy of *Haute Banque*

Éric Bussière

Haute Banque houses dominated the Paris marketplace during the first half of the 19th century. They were characterized primarily by the concentration of major resources into the hands of merchant families and were organized into international networks, with financial business and corporate sponsorships playing a major role.[1] The model appears to have exhausted its dynamic potential midway through the 19th century, when the major joint-stock banks, founded from the 1850s onwards, seem to have superseded *Haute Banque* in financing the economy.

It was not a mere and simple substitution however, but more like an overlaying onto the former structures by new ones, with the old institutions remaining as partners to the newer ones during a long period. The *Haute Banque* legacy therefore subsisted through the new banking institutions such as the Banque de Paris et des Pays-Bas (Paribas) and Comptoir national d'escompte de Paris (CNEP), the later having become BNP in 1966.

The change in dimension which occurred midway through the century appears to have been a vast consolidation operation among the business networks which reinforced their resources. The Paribas French investment banking model is closer to the *Haute Banque* model, in which it is more directly rooted. The major commercial banking model, involving a broad national and international network of branches, is further

---

1 Jérôme Greenfield, "Le Crédit mobilier avant la suprématie des Pereire," *Histoire, économie et société*, 2020/2, p. 46–63. Alain Plessis, "The Parisian *Haute Banque* and the international economy, in the nineteenth and the early twentieth centuries," in Youssef Cassis & Philip L. Cottrell (eds.), *The World of Private Banking*, Abingdon, Routledge, 2009, p. 153–166.

removed from the *Haute Banque* model, which it even appears to oppose by the nature of its business lines and the type of clientele it addresses.

However, a distinction between these two models was only clearly made after the 1889 crisis. Prior to this date, Paribas and CNEP shared certain common features, such as the origins of their founders and their types of business lines. The *Haute Banque* model prevailed within Paribas and was also present within CNEP until the 1889 crisis. The years following this crisis saw a specialization occur within the French banking system, with Paribas and CNEP adopting different complementary strategies. Changes over the ensuing decades appear to have definitively distanced these major banking institutions from the *Haute Banque* model. A more durable legacy than would appear subsists however within the structure, governance and business lines of these two institutions, as in the case of other major marketplace institutions.

1. During the founding period: *Haute Banque* as a genetic factor?

Paribas could be considered as the "offspring" of *Haute Banque*. Its founding in 1872 resulted from the combination of private banking houses of German origin located in the Netherlands, then in Belgium from the 1830s onwards.[2] The Bischoffsheim merchant family from Mainz played a prominent role by associating with the Goldschmidt, Bamberger and Cahen d'Anvers families and with Maurice de Hirsch in the following generation.

Paribas was created in two stages.[3] Firstly the Banque de crédit et de dépôt des Pays-Bas was set up in 1863 during the development of the Paris marketplace and the determination to consolidate the Bischoffsheim group banking houses in Paris and more broadly in Western Europe, in association with certain shareholders of Comptoir d'escompte de Paris

2 René Brion & Jean-Louis Moreau, *La Société générale de Belgique, 1822–1997*, Brussels, Fonds Mercator, 1998.

3 Éric Bussière, *Paribas, l'Europe et le Monde, 1872–1992*, Brussels, Fonds Mercator, 1992.

(founded in 1848),[4] including the Hentsch bankers from Geneva, who had been established in Paris since the 1810s.

The creation of Paribas in January 1872 corresponds to the association of this initial group with the Banque de Paris, which was founded in 1869 by a Parisian group and became a progressively more powerful competitor of Rothschilds. Paribas' creation was directly linked with the second bond issue launched to pay-off the war indemnities owed by France to Prussia in July 1872. Its creation therefore corresponded to the consolidation of a European network of *Haute Banque* houses brought together to undertake an international issue of historic proportions. This vast operation also marks the lasting alliance between these houses and the new generation of deposit banks set up in France since 1848, such as Comptoir d'escompte de Paris and Crédit lyonnais (in 1863).

In many ways the creation of Comptoir d'escompte de Paris resulted from a variety of circumstances and the combination of highly different founding groups. Its founding was attributable to the 1848 economic crisis and a government initiative to facilitate the resurgence of the credit market. The initiative therefore primarily involved a group of merchants from the Paris marketplace. Its business focused chiefly upon discounting bills involving a large number of operations, with a very broad range of clients each investing limited amounts of capital.

The identity of Comptoir d'escompte de Paris changed however during the 1860s, following the free trade treaty between France and UK, as it moved closer towards the world of *Haute Banque*: first, by creating an international network, but on a different basis from Paribas, by initially setting up branches and locating in distant sites; second, by diversifying its business lines, particularly the development of national and international financial operations; last, by forming ties with the founders of Société Générale in 1864 including Édouard Hentsch, the future founder of Paribas. It could therefore be asserted that the sea-change which took place in the banking industry mid-century, observed from the viewpoint of the major founders of BNP-Paribas, involved a convergence of the models in which *Haute Banque* played a central role. Paribas is primarily the result of a change in dimension and the

---

4 Nicolas Stoskopf, "Alphonse Pinard et la révolution bancaire du Second Empire," *Histoire, économie et société*, 1998/2, p. 299–317. Nicolas Stoskopf, *Les patrons du Second Empire. Banquiers et financiers parisiens*, Paris, Picard 2002.

consolidation of the *Haute Banque* model, although Paribas operated in a symbiotic relationship, from its foundation onwards, with the new credit institutions arising from the banking revolution during the Second Empire.

Although Comptoir d'escompte de Paris was originally based more on the latter model, it adopted a profile which bore greater resemblance to *Haute Banque* during the 1860s. The *Haute Banque* community appears therefore to be more of a modernizing factor among financial institutions, rather than an outdated model destined to disappear.

2. *Haute Banque* in practice in the 1870s–1880s

The legacy of *Haute Banque* appeared to consolidate during these two decades and not to have become outdated. Paribas adopted a model based on financial activities, centred on security issues used to fund governments, territorial authorities and utilities. These activities were developed on an international scale, with the breakdown of the securities portfolio in 1890 as follows: France 15 %, Europe 34 %, Latin America 28 %, and the Middle East 18 %. The activities also included corporate financing, particularly in the manufacturing industry, which represented 25 % of the Paribas securities portfolio around 1890. A network of alliances was set up via correspondents throughout Europe and the rest of the world and strategic partnerships were also set up with major European and Western banks, while stakes were also taken in peripheral Europe.

The *Haute Banque* legacy grew through cautiously managed sponsorships and the extension of measures put in place for the 1872 French State loan and also via further major international issues. Within Comptoir d'escompte de Paris, the influence of the *Haute Banque* model consolidated under the Hentsch presidency during the period from 1874 to 1889. A type of convergence with the *Haute Banque* model occurred. Hentsch, who was one of the founders of Société générale[5] and Paribas, set up a partnership with Paribas from 1870 to 1880.

The business activities of Comptoir d'escompte de Paris were therefore similar to those of Paribas, including French and international issues

---

5 Hubert Bonin, *Histoire de la Société générale*, tome I : *1864–1890. Naissance d'une banque moderne*, Geneva, Droz, 2006. Hubert Bonin, *Histoire de la Société générale*, tome II : *1890–1914. Une grande banque française*, Geneva, Droz, 2019.

funding government states and utilities in the Mediterranean region and Latin America, corporate sponsorship and developing international partnerships. There was one main difference however. The structure of the international network diverged greatly and was characterized by its transversal profile ranging from London and Paris to the Far East. The other difference was the start of a domestic network in France.

3. What was left of this model and its convergence after the 1889 crisis of Comptoir d'escompte de Paris?

The 1889 crisis led to a segmentation of the business activities. The reorganization of Comptoir d'escompte de Paris – which became Comptoir national d'escompte de Paris between 1889 and 1966 – was based on the French commercial banking model involving a national network, short-term financing business and the issuance of French and international securities, limited chiefly to security placements among the existing clientele.

Complementary CNEP's operations were also consolidated with investment banking activities, thus determining a specialization within the French banking system.

Meanwhile, Paribas, on the other hand, saw its model consolidate until 1914 with an initial inflexion towards the mixed banking model from 1890 to 1900. This tendency became discernible once more from the war period onwards.

On its side, one might ponder what was left of *Haute Banque* after 1890. Paribas appears to have carried the legacy of *Haute Banque* for a longer period, with no network and long-term corporate financing, albeit on a much larger scale.

Specialization of the banking system was consolidated by the two world wars and the Second World War banking laws, when specialization became the norm.

A few *Haute Banque* characteristics proved more durable. *Haute Banque* houses remained durably present at the heart of the Paribas system until the period between the two world wars. The Paribas model was replicated by BUP (Banque de l'Union parisienne)[6] with protestant *Haute Banque* houses from 1904 onwards. The pattern for recruiting managers

6 Hubert Bonin, *La Banque de l'Union parisienne (1874/1904–1974) De l'Europe aux Outre-mer*, Paris, Société française d'histoire des outre-mers-SFHOM, 2011.

extended the *Haute Banque* tradition, with Emile Ullmann as the deputy CEO of CNEP, of German origin, who had close economic ties with Germany and concentrated business activities on international deals. Similarly, Horace Finaly,[7] at Paribas, of Hungarian origin, was recruited from private banking but reflected the progressive transition towards the profile of salaried managing directors at Paribas.

International culture had ever been at the heart of the Paribas culture, resisting against the withdrawal into national interest by the French economy and the 1946 nationalization, thanks to the determination of its managers and the French government to preserve the international profile of French finance. This culture is reflected by the rapid return by Paribas to the international market via the Euromarkets and thanks to major international alliances based on the pre-1914 model. This culture also appears through the European banking clubs during the 1960s for commercial banks such as CNEP and then BNP, and also through permanent personal links underpinning international strategies.

So, rather than a simple reference to a distant mythical past, the legacy of the *Haute Banque* subsists through a culture[8] which continually adapts itself to the current economic and institutional situation.

---

7 Éric Bussière, *Horace Finaly, banquier, 1871–1945*, Paris, Fayard, 1996.

8 See: Youssef Cassis & Philip Cottrell, *Private Banking in Europe: Rise Retreat and Resurgence*, Oxford, Oxford University Press, 2015.

Chapter 5

The history of Banque de Neuflize OBC (1667–2017)

Ton de Graaf

The bank Neuflize, Schlumberger, Mallet OBC (NSM) whose history goes back to 1667, the date on which the David André banking house, the precursor of De Neuflize banking house, was established in Genoa is the oldest Parisian bank.[1] NSM is the result of successive mergers between the three founding banking houses De Neuflize, Schlumberger, Mallet.[2] NSM took part and still takes part today in France's banking and industrial development. Anxious to perfect the services offered, the three founding banks of NSM successfully anticipated and favoured the major socio-economic changes by founding what were at the time new companies such as the Banque de France, the railway or insurance companies which are examples of the enterprising spirit of these financial houses.

Each of these three banks had its own particular history, initiatives and preferences but nevertheless, all three had common characteristics which made their merger in 1966 an economic success. As family businesses, they were set up as general partnerships with the joint responsibilities of the managing associates until 1966, the date of the transformation of NSM into a limited liability company. This choice of legal structure is the result of a cultural phenomenon: loyal to their Protestant faith, the André, De Neuflize, Schlumberger and Mallet families were forced to emigrate for religious reasons and therefore had to

---

1 Christian Grand, *Trois siècles de banque. De Neuflize, Schlumberger, Mallet, de 1667 à nos jours*, Paris, E/P/A éditions, 1991.

2 Herbert Lüthy, *Mallet frères et Cie : 250 ans de banque*, Paris, Cujas, 1963.

leave their home province. From this exile, these families kept the very strong sentiment of belonging to an international minority, reserving the management of the banking house to members of their family or to close relatives up until the 1960s.

As French banks, the De Neuflize, Schlumberger and Mallet firms have, for over three hundred years, witnessed both the happy events and misfortunes of France and Europe without ever having failed in their commitments. The De Neuflize, Schlumberger and Mallet associates managed prestigious companies (the chairmanship of the AGF insurance group, the Eaux d'Évian mineral water company, the Paris-Lyon-Méditerranée (PLM) railway company, the Huaron copper mines, etc.) and in the same way with their personnel displayed courage during the wars and periods of economic crisis.

Through a series of examples, this chapter will endeavour to give a brief description of these firms before they took the clear-sighted decision to concentrate their strengths in one company, NSM. A guardian of their principles of work, uprightness and solidarity, this private bank with an international vocation is the French subsidiary of ABN AMRO bank.

1. The stages of growth of a bunch of *Haute Banque* houses

Several families of bankers undertook to develop business strategies to take profit of opportunities of growth throughout the various political regimes from the end of the 17th century to the take-off of the first industrial revolution and of the first banking revolution altogether.

A. First, the founding families seeking refuge abroad

Under the *Ancien Régime* – the monarchy regime in the 17th and 18th centuries – the severe repression of the Counter-Reformation – against the Protestants, from 1685 – forced the young members of the Mallet, André, Poupart (de Neuflize) and Schlumberger families to seek refuge abroad to found their families in peace without fear of seeing them wiped out. In the 15th century, Nicolas Schlumberger from Setzingen found refuge in Guebwiller, in the *République libre of Mulhouse*, a town in the eastern part of France which was an independent republic at the time.

In 1557, Jacques Mallet, from Rouen, settled in Geneva where he was given the position of "Bourgeois", a title granting the rights and privileges of the city. In 1667, David André from Nîmes founded his trading and banking firm in the free port of Genoa and finally, in the year 1710, Jean Abraham Poupart (de Neuflize) left Paris for the principality of Sedan. At this time, these three families formed part of the European class of Protestant merchants in which family and commercial relations were closely linked.

B. The André and Mallet companies under the Ancien Régime

Refusing all financial activity linked to the public finances of the realm, these two houses carried out their business in banking activities and speculation in merchandise just like all the merchant bankers at the time. The banking activities consisted of the usual processing of bills of exchange, the receipt of revenues from customers' private investments and more complicated operations on foreign exchange arbitrage and advances on cargos. The end of the 18th century saw the extension of commercial discount in Europe which was widely practiced by the two houses whose correspondents were practically all first class trading companies.

Despite the speed and efficiency with which the banking operations were executed, the low commissions could not suffice to maintain the families of the associates and their personnel. They therefore coupled these with commercial activities which were more profitable. The André house traded mainly in cereals and oils in the Mediterranean under the *Ancien Régime* with broking activities in merchandise, trading assisted by a fleet of some ten coasting vessels. For the Mallet house, established in Paris in 1713, in addition to the usual speculative operations in merchandise, the trading in luxury products sold principally to the *Gardes suisses de Paris* (the King's personal guards) guaranteed the firm its necessary additional revenues.

The reputation of the two companies guaranteed their continual growth and, in the 1780s, they ranked first with a promising future. This did not prevent the Mallet bankers from risking this position by committing themselves politically with Voltaire in the Calas affair whose widow they lodged during the rehabilitation proceedings in 1765. In the years to follow, the two bankers were to be confronted with the reign of Terror and its disruption of the economy.

C. The French Revolution: A time of hardship

Although the Declaration of the Rights of Man and the Citizen was greeted with interest by the associates, the Revolution was to cost the André and Mallet firms and the Neuflize cloth manufacture considerable hardship and expense. Due to the galloping depreciation of the *assignats* (banknotes used during the French Revolution) and the ensuing economic stagnation, their banking and commercial activities went into a dormant period from 1792 to 1800. The prohibition of joint stock companies added to the drop in income borne particularly by the loss of the Mallet firm's shares in the first Compagnie des eaux de Paris (Paris water company) and in the Caisse d'escompte (discount house).

In Paris, the *Comité de Salut public* (an organ of the Revolutionary Government) ordered the arrest of all the bankers on the market as suspects, and the three Mallet associates were imprisoned for many months at the *Collège du Plessis*.[3] To avoid having to go out of business, the wives of the three associates, with the help of Charpentier,[4] the *fondé de pouvoirs* (administrative officer), assured the day to day management of affairs. Thanks to their efforts, the Mallet house was one of the rare Parisian banks of the *Ancien Régime* to have survived the Revolution. Freed after the fall of Maximilien de Robespierre, the Mallet associates were keen to protect to the poorly handled interests of their private income customers. With banker Jean-Frédéric Perregaux, they formed the *Association Pérignon*, which was a property investment company before the term existed as the stockholders paid their government bonds into a common fund to have them converted into purchases of farms in Belgium which had been confiscated from the French nobility and clergy during the Revolution.

In Genoa, the period of adversity came with the proclamation of the Republic of Liguria (a state substituted for the Republic of Genoa in

3 See Alain Plessis, "La Révolution et les banques en France: de la Caisse d'escompte à la Banque de France" in *Revue économique*, volume 40, n° 6, 1989, p. 1001-1014 and Nicolò Valmori, "Les origines d'un malentendu tragique: les banquiers et la Révolution française", in *Annales historiques de la Révolution française*, 2017/2 (n° 388), p. 53-74.

4 His subname cannot be found in the archives.

1797 and incorporated into the French Empire in 1805) which did away with the commercial advantages of the free port, illusory in a period of such grave economic crisis. With the French Consulate, Dominique André, important creditor of the French State to which he had supplied 10,000 tons of cereals, decided to establish the bank in Paris in 1800, judging that the conditions of life and religious freedom were satisfactory and that the attempts to have his loans reimbursed would be easier to make. Unfortunately, his efforts were in vain.

2. The industrial development of the 19th century: The activities of the André and Mallet firms in France and abroad

Although weakened, the two houses came through the bloody upheavals of the Revolution and the scandals of the *Directoire*, unscathed.[5] Benefiting on this account from a revival of renown, their associates then played an increasingly exemplary financial role in the issue of French or foreign bonds and the sale of shares and bonds to the public. Alongside the traditional banking operations already mentioned, private asset management became a speciality of the two houses.

Their trading activities gradually took second place (wholesale trade in soaps and salts in the Mallet warehouses at Bercy, along the Seine harbour; American cotton for the André house), before disappearing altogether in the 1850s, investments in the industrial or service sectors being increasingly preferred. Investments in the aforementioned sectors were the major innovation in the general management strategy of the two houses, their reserves formerly having been invested in Government stock or cash deposits. With the participation of Guillaume Mallet in the founding of the Banque de France in 1800, many new companies were to be formed. Investing in new economic sectors like insurance or railways, the Mallet and the André families gave the initial impetus, with numerous other bankers at this time, to whole sectors of the French and even European economies. Battling against the prejudices of

5 See: Louis Bergeron, *Banquiers, négociants et manufacturiers parisiens du Directoire à l'Empire*, Paris, Ehess-Mouton, 1978. Bertrand Gille, *La banque et le crédit en France de 1815 à 1848*, Paris, Puf, « Mémoires & documents publiés par l'École des chartes, tome xiv », 1959.

a conservative administration, these associates were to play an active role in the Assurances générales French insurance group from 1819, the year it was established,[6] in the first railway companies in 1840–1850, in the canals, etc.

Their role in the urbanization of Paris is also worthy of note: anticipating the future of the department stores, the Mallet bankers were the first, in 1827, to build a shopping arcade in metal, the *Galerie de Fer* which was followed by another Mallet project: the *passage Choiseul* and the *Théâtre royal de l'Opéra comique.* A very important property development at the time was the *quartier Faubourg Poissonière* which was serviced and developed by the André firm, in charge of this project for nearly thirty years.

However, their functions as *Régents* (directors) of Banque de France, as well as bankers or company chairmen did not make the associates forget their social duties: every year, they redistributed part of their profits to their personnel and to benevolent funds. During the Greek War of Independence in the 1820s, the André firm dispatched provisions and drugs free of charge to the Christian Greeks, and they took part with the Delessert and Mallet firms in the founding of the Caisse d'épargne de Paris (savings bank) in 1818. As for the Mallet firm, the Paris infant schools and *écoles normales* (to educate future teachers) were founded by Émilie Mallet (née Oberkampf) with the funds of the bank and the assistance of Minister François Guizot, an ancestor of the Schlumberger family. Mallet participated in the railway construction wave, as also did André. They participated in the railways Lille-Strasbourg-Basel, Paris-Lyon, Paris-Orléans. André was also active in the railways of metropolitan Paris suburbs.

In 1855, Mallet and André were engaged in the establishing of the Grand Hôtel du Louvre for the World Exhibition. Gustave Girod, later partner in Banque André, started in 1859 the mineral water company in Évian-les-Bains. De Neuflize participated in the founding of the Banque impériale ottomane in 1863. After the Franco-German War in 1871, Alfred André, of Neuflize, was charged with the negotiation of the indemnities due to Germany: the bank floated loans which made

---

6 Born in 1816, the Assurances générales group was authorized by the *Conseil d'État* to practice fire insurance and life insurance and to act on foreign markets on October 20, 1819.

it possible to accelerate the liberation of the territories lost to Germany during the war. Mallet was involved in the Paris urban development works undertaken by *Préfet* Georges Haussmann. In 1871 the bank contributed to the great success of the large loans that were floated for the reconstruction of the country after the German invasion.

In 1879, Albert Mallet joined the board of Compagnie générale des eaux (set up in 1853) for water utilities. In 1904, the bank took part in the establishment of the Banque de l'Union parisienne,[7] the successor of Banque parisienne, which drew a community of merchant banks to extend its scope. On the eve of World War I, the bank of Mallet Frères & Cie had largely contributed to the establishment and spread of industry throughout France.

3. The interwar period: A period of adaptation and modernization

With the end of the First World War, the *Belle Époque* period also came to a close along with the *franc germinal* (the French franc adopted in the year 1800) and the rural world. With the development of communications and faster technological progress, banking methods changed and the Schlumberger company is a perfect illustration. Established in 1919 through the association of three friends, Maurice Schlumberger, André Istel and Louis Noyer, the SIN company was soon using a punch card system to process customers' orders.

Specialized like its colleagues in private asset management, it went further by creating a financial research department and the first French investment company called Gestion mobilière. The important customers companies and private individuals eventually put their trust in these young men, whereas between the two world wars, the other two banks were deprived of a certain number of posts of administrator by the wave of nationalizations in 1936 which affected Banque de France and the railway companies.

---

[7] Hubert Bonin, *La Banque de l'union parisienne (1874/1904–1974). De l'Europe aux outre-mers*, Paris, Publications de la Sfhom, 2011.

4. The wars: A dormant period for business

Bearing the patriotic spirit, the associates and the personnel had a firm attitude during the wars: the refusal to collaborate in any way with the enemy and the active role in the war economy. When they weren't soldiers, they took on important assignments: the negotiation of *Libération* loans in 1815 by the Mallet and André firms; the 1870 *Libération* loan by Alfred André and Léon Say[8]; the mission to New York in 1915 of the *Régent* of Banque de France Ernest Mallet, who negotiated the considerable loan of 200 million dollars for France which had been bled white; at the end of the Second World War, André Istel took part in the Bretton Woods agreements.

During the Second World War, as France was occupied by the German army and administration, the banks had to apply measures dictated by the occupier or the Vichy regime. The leaders of the different houses behaved more than honourably in these difficult times. They tried as far as they could to protect the assets of their clients, especially those targeted by the anti-Jewish laws. At Schlumberger et Cie, André Istel, as a Jew, had to go into exile in the US and became a financial advisor to the Free French.[9]

In terms of banking activity, these periods of occupation represented a dormant period, only the day today management being assured. However, following the law organizing the banking profession in 1941, banks had to opt for one of three statuses: merchant bank, deposit bank, or medium and long-term credit bank. Like many other *Haute banque* houses, Neuflize, Schumberger and Mallet opted for the status of deposit bank, which forced them, especially Neuflize, to dispose of a large part of their shareholdings in companies.

---

8 See: Arthur Monroe, "The French indemnity of 1871 and its effects," *The Review of Economics and Statistics*, October 1919, volume 1, no. 4, p. 269–281 (*Jstor*).

9 The three sons of Maurice Schlumberger chose the right side and paid for it in their own lives: Georges died in the ranks of the Free French, Xavier died during his deportation and Rémy was wounded in the ranks of the French army. At Mallet's, Jean-Pierre Mallet (1915–2003) managed funds for escape networks of pilots and secret agents (Christian Grand, *op. cit*, p. 205–213).

5. Since 1945, the advantages of the mergers: Renewing the *Haute Banque* legacy

After the Second World War, the need of concentration of the banking industry became increasingly obvious, as the banking trade came to involve too much capital for one family bank. The first mergers took place in 1945 between the De Neuflize and Schlumberger banks, and was to end quite logically in 1966 with the entry of a third house bearing the same *Haute Banque* traditions: the Mallet company. At the time, the directors had anticipated the development of the European banking market and wanted to broaden NSM's position on an international level, with, in 1967, a stake in the Swiss Neue Bank, and in 1968, crossed participations with the German bank Delbrück & Co. From 1970 to 1971, NSM began negotiations with Bank Mees & Hope, a renowned bank in Amsterdam and a correspondent of NSM for over 150 years which ended with the Dutch bank taking a stake in the capital of NSM.

A few years later, ABN Bank took over the control of Bank Mees & Hope. Rather than buying back the Dutch stake when it had the means to do so, NSM confirmed its agreement by consenting to join its present partner and confirmed it with the merger in 1980 of another private family bank Banque Jordaan in Paris. At the same time ABN Bank acquired a majority stake in NSM.

After 1990, ABN AMRO – resulting from a merger between ABN Bank and AMRO Bank[10] – did several acquisitions in France. In 1997, Demachy Worms & Cie (set up in 1798)[11] was acquired, before this bank merged with NSM in 1999. In 1998, Banque du Phénix, established in 1958, merged with NSM. In 2006, Neuflize OBC was created by the merger of OBC (Odier, Bungener & Courvoisier, dating back to 1785) with Banque de Neuflize.

Following the ABN AMRO merger in 1991, the merchant bank Neuflize OBC benefitted from a planetary banking network which it can

---

10 Johan De Vries, Wim Vroom & Ton de Graaf (eds.), *Worldwide Banking. ABN AMRO Bank, 1824–1999*, Amsterdam, ABN AMRO Bank, 1999.

11 Jean-François Belhoste & Henri Rouquette, La *maison Seillière-Demachy, banque de l'industrie et du commerce depuis le XVIIIe siècle*, Paris, 1977 (published by the bank).

use for its business and private customers. Thus, backed by a European bank but maintaining its own corporate culture and traditions, Banque Neuflize OBC continuity has been guaranteed, balancing the legacy of *Haute Banque* and the building of a competitive future.

Chapter 6

A part of the legacy of *Haute Banque*? The asset management business in France at the beginning of the 21st century

LAURE QUENNOUËLLE-CORRE

The usual definition of *Haute Banque* contains different types of activities and consequently can be differently interpreted by historians. The term includes a wide range of financial professions: investment banking (mergers and acquisitions, underwriting); asset management and financial advices; wealth management and private banking. In this volume, Hubert Bonin puts the light on the French investment banking and the forever important role of merchant banks in M&A and underwriting activities. As he writes, "the 'legacy of finance' has therefore been preserved, revitalized and extended thanks to the rebirth of Lazard and Rothschild."[1]

But, compared to investment funds and big commercial banks, the two French investment banks keep currently a minor role in asset management and wealth management as well. And actually the fees gained from these latter activities compared to M&A are minor in their own turnover. That is that part of *Haute Banque*'s activities this chapter intends to explore. As financial globalization has been expanding during the last three decades, the development of new financial products and capital markets involved different kind of financial players. It seems interesting to bring out the possible revival of a part of the legacy of *Haute Banque* through asset management and wealth management activities.

---

1 Hubert Bonin, "French *Haute Banque*: From the legacy to the revival since the 1980s," in this volume.

The pending issue to discuss here includes two key questions. First, did successors of *Haute Banque* practice the same trades as they did in a very different economic and financial environment? Can we identify a part of legacy in the new professions in asset management, wealth management, private banking, whereas the whole banking and financial organization has completely changed? Second, can we make a difference – or not – between the former personal relationships and the modern social networking in the era of the second financial globalization? This question is suggested by the conference's special issue about the current lack of personal relationships between customers and banks.

1. A quick reminder of *Haute Banque* in the 19th century

Before trying to compare the two periods of financial globalization, we have to define clearly what the *Haute Banque* in France at the time was. The starting point of the conference was that at the time, "*Haute Banque* institutions were well respected and dealt with major international business and state affairs." But who were those private bankers who made up the *Haute Banque?* Without going back before the Revolution, the French or Swiss *Haute Banque* included a group of private banks located in Paris in the middle of the 19th century.[2] The world referred to a small number of "private" houses established in Paris: these were sometimes individual businesses, but more often a partnership, usually organized as a general partnership. These small banks used both their own assets and the assets of several wealthy families for their business; in fact, they were working with few own funds: less than ten million of francs for most of them. This definition of *Haute Banque* does include banks such as Perier, Laffitte, Vernes, Delessert, Mallet or Hottinguer; most of them were either French or Swiss, but also German or English …

2 See Alain Plessis, "The Parisian *Haute Banque* and the International economy in the nineteenth and early twentieth centuries," in Youssef Cassis and Philip Cottrell (eds.), *The World of Private Banking*, Abingdon, Routledge, 2009, p. 153–166. Pierre-Cyrille Hautcoeur and Georges Gallais-Hamonno (eds.), *Le marché financier français au XIXe siècle*, volume 1, Paris, Publications de la Sorbonne, 2007, chapter 1.

Since then, several historians have identified two types of *Haute Banque* from the early 19th century[3]: first of all, the industrial bankers, who invested in mining, steel industry, textile, and so on.[4] They were a minority which almost disappeared with the second industrial revolution. A second type comprised those who concentrated their activities on financial operations and securities transactions. The main trends of their strategies were diversifying of investments, searching a balance between risk and return, and having interest for medium-term investments in different sectors such as industry, insurance, public services, real estate.

In fact, throughout the 19th century, the most important areas of activity for the *Haute Banque* were focused on international trade financing, discounting activities, and issuing (especially Governments' loans, French or foreigner). Proximity to political and financial power was an important characteristic of the *Haute Banque*, such as being among the "*régents*" of Banque de France (Vernes, Mallet, Neuflize, Rothschild, Hottinguer, to mention only the best known).[5]

The strength of *Haute Banque* was based on the personal risks taken by individuals: therefore, the relevance of the reputation of banks and the links with governments characterized this banking sector.[6] In that regard, their local role based on personal relationships might have remained of importance at this time. They have certainly taken advantage of their functions at the central bank and of their close family ties in the world of industry and finance.[7]

But while the second industrial revolution emerged, the need for concentrated funds involved, the weakening of individual relationships

---

3 See David Landes, "Vieille banque et banque nouvelle. La révolution financière du XIXe siècle," *Revue d'histoire moderne et contemporaine*, 1956, tome 3, no. 3, p. 204–222. Nicolas Stoskopf, *Les patrons du Second Empire. Banquiers et financiers parisiens*, Paris, Picard, 2002. Jérôme Greenfield, "Le Crédit mobilier avant la suprématie des Pereire," *Histoire, économie & société*, 2020/2, p. 46–63.

4 Louis Bergeron, "Les espaces du capital," in André Burguière and Jacques Revel (eds.), *Histoire de la France. L'espace français*, Paris, Seuil, p. 307.

5 Alain Plessis, *Régents et gouverneurs de la Banque de France*, Geneva, Droz, 1985; *La politique de la Banque de France de 1851 à 1870*, Geneva, Droz, 1985.

6 Marc Flandreau and Juan Flores, "Bonds and brands: Foundations of sovereign debt markets, 1820–1830," *The Journal of Economic History*, 2009, volume 69, no. 3, p. 646–684.

7 Jean-Jacques Laurendon (pseudonym of Jean Bouvier), *Psychanalyse des banques*, Paris, Sedimo, 1964.

in financial and banking businesses and finally, the decline of *Haute Banque* as a major actor of the financial system and the birth of large commercial banks (joint-stocks companies).[8] The weakness of the *Haute Banque* appeared quickly as it could not provide enough capital flows to finance big projects and large investments, like railways or channels. The institutions were not able either to meet the needs of small and middle firms. Consequently, they have been competed by big joint-stock banks for investing in these capital-intensive industrial sectors. Even if the heads of these businesses were amongst the first to become interested in the new limited companies, none of them were ever tempted to transform their own banks into joint-stock companies.

After a time of glory, lots of local banks and small investment banks disappeared or were merged, whereas the biggest ones were still active, as H. Bonin explains in this volume about Rothschild and Lazard' success story. The Great Depression caused many bankruptcies including local banks and small merchant banks. Did the Interwar sound the end of this banking aristocracy? Or did they survive at the eve of the 21st century and in what form?

2. The development of wealth and asset management in France

Let us jump a few decades later, in the 1970s. After the end of the gold exchange standard and the re-opening of financial borders (end of exchange control), the second financial globalization has emerged, following the huge increase in the ensuing movement of capital flows. In France, for a long time, mutual funds have been banned. They were not considered as necessary, the pay-as-you-go pension system having been preferred to the funded pension system since 1945. It began to change in the sixties with the creation of two collective investment schemes, SICAV (mutual funds) and FCP (common investment funds/*fonds communs de placement*) and then in 1978, when the launch of *SICAV Monory* – after the name of a ministry of Finance in the 1970s – were launched with success. After that, deregulation and disintermediation opened up access to financial markets to savers and France became ten years later

[8] See Pierre-Cyrille Hautcoeur and Georges Gallais-Hamonno (eds.), *Le marché financier français au XIXe siècle*, *op. cit.*, chapter 7.

the champion of UCITS (undertaking for collective investment in transferable securities): in 1988, there were more than 800 SICAV and 3,000 FCP in France, which then holds almost half of the UCITS capitalization in the European Community.

At the end of the 1980s, the global financial and banking landscape completely changed. Credit becomes less profitable than financial activities, big commercial banks develop lucrative new trades in finance area at an international level: derivatives and futures products, asset management, private banking. In a multi-polar world, different kinds of funds sharing the marketplace of asset management emerged.

So, on this lucrative niche markets, universal banks competed with new institutions operating on a global scale, according to an institutional framework which can be summarized schematically as follows. First, the asset management department accounts for a significant share of the French big banks' profits. These actors hold a large part of asset management, contrary to other countries like the UK or the US, where pension funds, hedge funds and others are the dominant actors of the sector.

The market share of collective management reaches 60 % of the total and 84 % of the PEE (*Plans d'épargne entreprise*) and PERCO (*plans d'épargne pour la retraite collectifs*) are concentrated on four major banks and an insurer: Amundi, Natixis AM, BNP Paribas AM, CM-CIC AM et Axa IM (Amundi, the first French asset management company is 60 % owned by Crédit agricole).[9] For instance, at the group BNP Paribas, the division called "Investment Solutions" posted in 2012 6.2 billion of euros of revenues (in assets under management at €889 billion) . It brings together five professions: insurance (Cardif); BNP Paribas Securities Services; Private banking (BNP Paribas Wealth Management); Asset management (BNP Paribas Investment Partners); and BNP Paribas Real Estate

Looking at the specific French context, the asset management industry represents 627 asset management companies, including four French asset managers in the *Top 20 Global Ranking*, managing 3,600 € billion of assets – by 2020, total assets under management in France amounted to nearly 4,185 billion euros – and working for individual investors or collective investment schemes. The French asset management industry,

9 The following information is taken from Sébastien Galanti and Françoise Le Quéré, "Industrie de la gestion d'actifs : de l'émergence à l'apparition de nouveaux risques," *Revue d'économie financière*, 2020/1, no. 137, p. 109–128.

one of the most dynamic in Europe, belongs to the core of the financial ecosystem[10]: France offers the second asset management largest pool in the world which represents 20 % of the European asset management industry. Entrepreneurial companies like Oddo, *OFI* (Ofivalmo, created in 1971, then OFI AM since 2006),[11] Carmignac, Financière de l'Échiquier operate both in private asset management and in collective asset management.

Nevertheless, the French asset management industry is still a dwarf next to the American giants. For instance, BlackRock, the most important multinational investment management, considered as the most influential financial institution in the world, announced more than five trillion $ under asset management in 2017, that is far more than the whole French asset management and banking departments ... Apart from the latter, the French firms are in competition in the European continent with global players such as Soros fund management or Carlyle.

Institutional investors (pension funds, insurance companies, banks) offered very safe investments (bonds) like life insurance, a very popular investment in France because of the tax exemption. They managed currently between 1,300 and 1,400 billion euros. In the area of wealth management or private asset management, "family offices" occupied a small but not negligible niche. They managed the wealth of very rich families (over 15 million euros). They were based on the diversification of assets: real estate, startups, art, financial products. About thirty family offices are active in France, with 21 % of investments in private equity, and 18 % in real estate.[12]

3. Discussion about the legacy of *Haute Banque*

Here is the current situation in France. Private banking and asset management are scattered among different types of institutions, so far from the former *Haute Banque*, at least in appearance. As we have seen before, some parts of the former businesses of *Haute Banque* still exist

---

10 See Laure Quennouëlle-Corre, "Paris: The possibility of revival as an international financial centre," in Youssef Cassis and Dariusz Wójcik (eds.), *International Financial Centres after the Global Financial Crisis and Brexit*, Oxford, Oxford University Press, 2018.

11 Website: [Groupe OFI (ofi-am.fr)].

12 Source: Association française du *Family Office* (AFFO).

nowadays: private banking and wealth management, asset management, are terms that cover the trades of the past. We can identify some similar trends in trades from one century to the next.

A. A part inherited from the past

As it was the case in the 19th century, the private banking and asset management are now based on the diversification of investments, thanks to the innovation process in progress since the 1980s: on the lookout for new opportunities, researching diversified financial products and investment in innovative sectors such as "green finance" is one of the specificities of asset management. Compared to UCITS, a "made to measure" service is their trump card. In fact, private banking and family offices propose a mix of direct investment and management under mandate.

At the first financial globalization, internationalization of investment (i.e. colonial trade) was one of the strengths of French banks, thanks to their wide network with the business community. The second globalization brings new opportunities to develop global products and services as well. In that regard, similar strategies in private banking have been held from 19th to 20th century.

For these dynamic capitalists, limited risks and high profitability remain important investment criteria as well. Can the timid appearance of venture capital and development capital in the 1980s in France be compared to the boldness of a Pereire or a Mallet which supported new sectors at the time? It is difficult to decide here. Nevertheless, the main difference lies in the much more developed pooling of risks at present.

Do personal relationships still matter? Undoubtedly private asset management and family offices rely on this type of personalized relationships to attract their customers. Here we can see that the "spirit" of *Haute Banque* is still alive. Family offices are looking for greater proximity to the companies in which they invest and wish to participate in real entrepreneurial stories. On the contrary, in collective asset management (big banks, pension funds), it appears as a minor aspect of the customer service.

To sum up, the main part of investment management has changed over time. They now have to choose among a large range of investments, especially collective investment undertakings and the managers are still their clients' advisors as formerly. Yet as these professionals are allowed to employ financial derivatives' instruments, asset management has become a profession that requires increasingly technical and even mathematical skills – although helped with automated trading programs. That job is very different from what it used to be two centuries ago, when *banquiers* were mostly skilful generalists, both wise and intuitive advisors.

Although similarities have been identified in the field of private banking from one century to the next, however the eco-financial system and the institutional environments have dramatically changed and have modified altogether the profession, the spirit, and the organization of firms. Is there still room for *Haute Banque*?

B. A new financial architecture

Globalization and liberalization of the financial area involved a series of transformation of the financial system. The second globalization involved a degree of integration never achieved before, thanks to the technological revolution coupled with a total liberalization of markets and the opening up of monetary and financial boundaries. Here comes an unstable and volatile era whereas numerous crises have also broken out along the 19th century, when small banks went bankrupt. But the current highly competitive world of actors is showing some very new signs in various fields.

The asset management industry benefited from banking disintermediation: assets under management grew throughout the 1990s, particularly from 1997 onwards. Supporting the dramatic development of collective management held by big banks or investment funds, institutional investors have become heavyweights in asset management. That is particularly true in France, where insurance companies prefer investing in bonds rather than equities: 50 % of the overall asset allocation of the French asset management is invested in bonds and 13 % in cash or monetary instruments, compared with 11 only 20 % in equities at the end of 2017.[13] This type of investors did not count as much before.

Another crucial point is the ascent of private equity industry (venture and development capital) which certainly weighs less than the credit or the stock market in terms of volume of capital, but which is crucial for

---

13 Sébastien Galanti, Françoise Le Quéré, "Industrie de la gestion d'actifs: de l'émergence à l'apparition de nouveaux risques" *op. cit.*

invest management in new firms. In France, the private equity industry was for a long time limited and developed from the years 1990 to 2000 with the multiplication of LBOs. Its recent growth in France was due to private and public actors: the State, Caisse des dépôts et consignations, BpiFrance, set up in 2012 from a merger of three public financial companies, etc. This public intervention is a new deal inside the French financial system far from the liberal organization in progress in the 19th century.

The nature of financial products changed significantly. For forty years, a very large choice of products, and among them, future markets (derivatives, option) burst out: in 2016, the outstanding number of derivatives is over one million billion dollars, more than the world stock markets. "Futures" are backed by clearing houses, which become a major issue for the capital markets.[14] The rise of algorithmic trading and the domination of derivatives' markets over equity markets are obviously elements that are disrupting the role of finance in the economy, compared to former financial systems.

Lastly, the development of new technologies and processes has recently turned the world of finance upside down: from digital trading to block chain is an ongoing challenge for the whole finance area (fintech, block chains …) and also affects the asset management industry. Alongside institutional investors who are increasing the weight of management companies, new players have recently emerged that are not management companies (online brokerage platforms, etc.). That is more and more difficult to regulate a constantly changing world.

4. Conclusion

New actors, new products, new processes, new environments: this time is really different, and it is a challenge for historians to make this leap in time without anachronisms. The nature of globalization has changed and the actors too. Indeed, like 150 years ago, a multi-polar world was reborn inhabited with segmented financial activities, but the actors are so different. In that regard, *Haute Banque* disappeared as an organization but the job and the spirit still exist here and there. Its representatives are

---

[14] In the 19th century, futures markets did not have such a sophisticated clearing system.

no longer "advisors to the Prince," they have no more close links with State neither with industrial firms. On the contrary, the financial legislation - the "Chinese wall" - forces them to separate investment activities and client advice. More generally, among the French bankers, few have been able to adapt to changes in the economic and financial environments (Rothschild and Lazard). Only they have succeeded to keep their name and their capital, but their profession has completely changed.

Studying the legacy of *Haute Banque* leads us to think about the change in the global financial system that has taken place over the past forty years. First, international capital flows have changed of direction and of economic impact. Finance has become disconnected from the real economy and capital flows are no longer based on real savings as they were before 1914. The volume of capital remains the same but it is disconnected with real savings, as Anton Brenden wrote: "Yesterday, the meaning of savings movements was linked first of all to the difference in the economic development of countries; today, it is more related to their financial development."[15] The financialization of developed economies completely upset the relationship between finance and economy and society.

Secondly, the centre of the world has shifted from Europe to the United States and Asia. France's role in the IFC has dramatically diminished and it is now only a stakeholder in the EU financial area. As a corollary, French and Swiss bankers are now a minor player in the global financial system. Lastly, the biggest difference probably lies in the new place of international regulators in investment banking and capital development since the 20th century, whereas banking system's regulation and organization is more or less under enhanced control of central banking.

---

[15] Anton Brender and Florence Pisani, *Les déséquilibres financiers internationaux*, Paris, La Découverte, 2007, p. 23.

Chapter 7

French *Haute Banque*: From the legacy to the revival since the 1980s

Hubert Bonin

Investment banking in France in the years 1980s–2010s is often exemplified by the remnants of *Haute Banque* houses: Lazard, Rothschild I and Rothschild II, beyond the giant armies of big universal banks. They endured upheavals, but then managed their rebirth and reached competitiveness, along three main paths towards M&A management, wealth management, and asset management. We intend thus to focus on the changes on the Paris market place at the turn of the 21st century, to gauge the balance between the heritage and the present evolution, in the wake of our researches on bankers[1] and investment banks.[2]

We will scrutinize three main issues, focused on the decline and rebirth of merchant banking in France. French merchant banks (*Haute Banque*) (Vernes, Hottinguer, NSM, etc.) met a financial and commercial ceiling in the 1970s–1980s, because of issues of family successions, banking nationalizations and restructurings, and the building of strong big groups that left shrink areas for small institutions. They disappeared, or were amalgamated within bigwigs, whilst American investment banks took step on the European places themselves.

---

1 Hubert Bonin, *Le monde des banquiers français au XXe siècle*, Brussels, Complexe, 2000. See: Youssef Cassis & Éric Bussière (eds.), *London and Paris as International Financial Centres in the Twentieth Century*, Oxford, Oxford University Press, 2005.

2 Hubert Bonin & Carlo Brambilla (eds.), *Investment Banking History. National and Comparative Issues (19th-21st Centuries)*, Brussels, Peter Lang, "Euroclio. Studies and Documents," 2014.

Big banks somewhat "swallowed" the culture of merchant banking, through Europeanization, solid offshoots in the City, Luxembourg and Geneva, the merger between Paribas and BNP, the integration of managerial cultures oriented towards relational banking on an international scale, their involvement in strong M&A practices. "*Banque d'affaires*" et "*banque de conseil*" (investment banking; consulting banking) were thus deeply incorporated within "universal banks," whilst the portfolio of skills in asset and wealth management found a large position in a few big European banks.

Anyway, merchant banking did resist such a corporate tsunami. Family or personalized *maisons de Haute Banque* – merchant banking houses (Lazard, Rothschild) – revolutionized their mode of management; they Europeanized and even globalized their strategic scope and business model. Their portfolio of knowledge in M&A management got much enriched, as a crucial niche within the reshuffling of international and French corporate business. Wealth management and asset management regained momentum along fresh ways of relationship, connections, technical tool-boxes, in competition with giants like UBS or big French banks. Two Rothschild groups and Lazard re-conquered first-ranking positions, whilst some houses adopted some profiles of the ex-merchant banks, when the culture of "boutiques" emerged in the Paris place. Last, big groups succeeded sometimes to respect and develop relevant affiliates, like Neuflize for ABN AMRO or 1819 for BPCE, as if the concept of merchant banking was no longer so much old-fashioned.

The rebirth of merchant banking cultures, within business units of big groups, autonomous affiliates of universal banks, or moreover at the heart of thoroughly renewed *Haute Banque* houses will thus be reconstituted and assessed, ever with a comparative path because of the issues about the competitiveness of the French marketplace against Italy, Switzerland, Luxembourg, Germany or the City.

This chapter will be a mere essay, relying of various sources, fare from any comprehensive and long study, as we did not delve into specialized printed or digital magazines like *Dealogics*, *Option Finance*, *Thomson-Reuters* or else. Our core intent is to seize the main issues and to assess the responses brought by this *Haute Banque* houses to preserve the legacy of previous generations.[3]

---

[3] We also thank Pierre Tattevin (and Victoire Grux) at Lazard, and the late Patrick

1. Tempests and uncertainties

Many factors contributed to foster uncertainties and upheavals among the community of French houses: the nationalizations move of 1982, the necessary relief of the big-wig leaders at the turn of the century, and the reshaping of the open economy.

A. The shock of nationalization for Rothschild in 1982–1984

The nationalization of Rothschild in 1982 put an end of almost two centuries of family banking[4]; but its business model had been questioned as it had added basic deposit banking to historical investment and private banking; its successor Européenne de banque itself was amalgamated into Barclays France in 1991. The Rothschild family had to restart from zero[5]; it had kept financial assets and sleeping shells, which were used as a basis for the rebuilding of a bank. The holding PO-Paris-Orléans, the name of which reminded of the railway company nationalized in 1937, was the lever to such a pyramid, altogether with the 440 million FRF of the indemnity paid for the nationalization of the bank. As soon as 1984, this PO tool originated a new bank, PO Bank, then Rothschild once more, which resumed the traditional activities of investment and private banking, whilst the family interests took place within the pyramidal structure. Then, in 2012, various assets were amalgamated within PO, which was transformed into Rothschild & Co, supervising the French bank. In the meanwhile, Lazard[6] escaped the nationalization because its

---

Ponsolle, an ex-Rothschild senior partner, for their interviews in the Spring 2017.

4 Derek Wilson, *Rothschild. A Story of Wealth and Power*, London, André Deutsch, 1988. John McKay, "The house of Rothschild (Paris) as a multinational industrial enterprise, 1875–1914," in Maurice Lévy-Leboyer (*et alii*, eds.), *Multinational Enterprise in Historical Enterprise*, Cambridge, Cambridge University Press, 1986, p. 74–86. Niall Ferguson, *The World's Banker. The History of the House of Rothschild*, London, Weidenfeld & Nicolson, 1998. Niall Ferguson, "The rise of the Rothschilds: The family firm as multinational," in Youssef Cassis & Philip Cottrell (eds.), *The World of Private Banking*, London, Ashgate, 2010, p. 1–30. Jean Bouvier, *Les Rothschild*, Paris, Fayard, 1967; second edition, Brussels, Complexe, 1985. Bertrand Gille, *Histoire de la maison Rothschild (1817–1870)*, Geneva, Droz, 1965 & 1967 [all books in Paris, except other locations].

5 Guy de Rothschild, *Contre bonne fortune*, Belfond, 1983, J'ai lu, 1985.

6 Martine Orange, *Ces Messieurs de Lazard*, Albin Michel, 2006. Anne Sabouret, *Lazard frères & compagnie, une saga de la fortune*, Olivier Orban, 2013 (first edition

deposits were under one billion FRF, as it had stuck to its classical business model (investment and private banking).

B. The issue of transgenerational shift

In both cases anyway the durability was questioned through the issue of the trans-generational shift. At Rothschild,[7] Guy de Rothschild (1909–2007) had been the boss after WWII (*associé-gérant* in 1945–1967, chairman in 1967–1982). The process of recreating a house was stake along the capabilities of his sons David (1942) and Éric (1967). The elder one seized the helm and assumed the will, strategy, and completion of the project; but his brother was associated – he had been trained since 1987 at a small Wall Street house, Wertheim & Co., before becoming *associé-gérant* at Rothschild in 1993. A second shift was necessary, and happily the family fed a successor, with the duo David and his son Alexandre de Rothschild (born in 1980).[8]

At Lazard bigwigs had retired (Felix Rohatyn in 1949–1997,[9] André Meyer) or recently reached retirement (Georges Ralli, Antoine Bernheim, even if keeping personal activities in Italy at Generali[10]). The charge to federate and animate a challenged house was borne by Michel David-Weill (born in 1932), the inheritor of a past star of the bank.[11] Active in the house from 1956, he was the chairman from 1975 till 2001, and thus the holder of the helm through challenging years, extending the scope of

---

in 1987). Laurent Chemineau, *L'incroyable histoire de Lazard frères: la banque qui règne sur le monde des affaires*, Paris, Assouline, 1998. Guy-Alain de Rougemont, *Lazard frères, banquiers des deux mondes (1840–1939)*, Paris, Fayard, 2011. William Cohan, *The Last Tycoons: The Secret History of Lazard*, New York, Doubleday, 2007.

7 See: Tristan Gaston-Breton, *La saga des Rothschild*, Paris, Tallandier, 2017. Martine Orange, *Rothschild, une banque au pouvoir*, Albin Michel, 2012.

8 Anne-Sylvaine Chassany & Jacqueline Simmons, "The Rothschild empire anoints an heir," *Business Week*, July 19, 2012.

9 Félix Rohatyn, *Un banquier dans le siècle*, Saint-Simon, 2011.

10 Pierre de Gasquet, *Antoine Bernheim : le parrain du capitalisme français*, Grasset, 2011. Pierre de Gasquet, "Antoine Bernheim: le bâtisseur de fortunes s'est éteint hier à l'âge de 87 ans," *Les Échos*, June 6, 2012.

11 Nicolas Stoskopf, "Dirigeants de la banque Lazard," in Jean-Claude Daumas, Alain Chatriot, Danièle Fraboulet & Hervé Joly (eds.), *Dictionnaire historique des patrons français*, Paris, Flammarion, 2010, p. 408–410.

Frenchie-family institution embedded in strong and ancient bourgeoisies and arts sponsorships, into a competitive open-minded company.

But himself had to be succeeded by Bruce Wasserstein in 2001 when the House had to gather further momentum and reach a more globalized and integrated modus vivendi, which led to infightings between both bosses.[12] In October 2004 M. David-Weill had to move to other financial (and arts sponsoring) activities, when the associates supported the project to transform Lazard into a listed bank, which was completed in May 2005. After crossing dire years (with losses in 2002–2004), it had to complete its globalized structure and mode of management, to welcome fresh recruits, and to jump into fresh markets (in technologies and areas), which was started by Wasserstein, till his death in October 2009. In France, a new generation has seized on the wheel at the start of the century, with Bruno Roger (recruited in 1954) as the chairman of Lazard France en 2002, when Matthieu Pigasse joined the house and became its CEO in 2010 – B. Roger being also the chairman of Global Investment Banking of Lazard Group.

To foster this permanent transgenerational shift, "these houses show a capacity to find super-high potential, that we attract to a fixed wage at a high level, as an investment, one 'hello bonus', millions of dollars to introduce contacts. David of Rothschild succeeded by attracting talents, such Sébastien Proto and Emmanuel Macron. The job consists in spotting talented people at the financiers of the administration, at the very good lawyers."[13]

C. *The issue of Europeanization and globalization*

The de-segmentation of financial and banking markets questioned the French basis of Rothschild and Lazard.

Transatlantic legacy at Lazard

That latter started the process of adapting to such open framework: as soon as 1984 it concluded with the Pearson group/family, which controlled Lazard UK, a partnership, thus fostering mutualization, whilst

12 Tristan Gaston-Breton, "David-Weill contre Wasserstein, un fauteuil pour deux," *Les Échos*, 8 juillet 2014.

13 Interview with a senior investment banker, April 2017.

the historical connections with Lazard US were preserved, all the more because M. David-Weill had been trained along an American banking culture overseas. The softening of the familial grip over Lazard Paris – that of David-Weill family, because of the failure of the step-son Édouard Stern to assume the succession – and Lazard US (through the Meyer family) led to a thorough change in structures and philosophy: an American leader, Bruce Wasserstein (1947–2009), became the head manager in 2001; the three houses merged into a single Lazard LLC as a limited company in March 2000; and in 2005, at the instigation of Wasserstein, managing director, Lazard Ltd was listed on the Stock Exchange.[14]

The power of very few leaders (Michel David-Weill, Wasserstein) has been deeply alleviated in the 21st century when the group evolved towards commonplace co-managerial practices – under the guidance of Kenneth Jacobs till after his appointment as CEO in 2009. Financial transactions being most of the time transnational today, teams work in an integrated way, by bringing in sectorial expertises besides their local know-how. No more a family business, Lazard preserved anyway its tradition of high-range managers (with about 120 *associés* in 2010) as partners of the revenues and profits. But the core management is located in New York, with the US supplying 45 % of the revenues, *vs* 25 % in France, with desks in Atlanta, Chicago, Houston and Los Angeles, to resist the big investment banks – and even French Matthieu Bucaille became chief financial officer in New York.

European legacy at Rothschild

On its side, Rothschild has cemented its trans-Channel historical life: both British and French houses merged – along a complex process – in 2012,[15] and the new company has become resolutely bi-national, from New Court (in the City of London) and *rue de Messine* (Paris 8th), even if the French family holds the helm nowadays. Family holdings (Rothschild Concordia SAS, Paris-Orléans as limited partnership company) oversee a banking holding, Concordia holding sarl, itself controlling Rothschild & Co Banque (in France, with Olivier Pécoux as chairman of the executive committee) and Rothschild Continuation Holdings,

14 Mathieu Pechberty, "Riches comme Lazard," *La Tribune*, May 4, 2010.

15 Elsa Conesa, "La banque Rothschild fait un pas de plus vers la création d'un groupe mondial," *Les Échos*, April 5, 2012.

in the UK and the rest of the world. Rationalization and internationalization were combined targets, with a centralized organization and management (covering a staff of 2,400), as a revolution to the legacy of the culture of partnership. All in all, Rothschild and Lazard converged towards a balance between a banking firm and the preservation of the role and influence of senior partners and *associés-gérants*.

Moreover, Rothschild extended its non-European stretch. On one side, like Lazard, it set up *bureaux* in the Middle East to entice local rich or institutional investors to orient capitals towards Europe. On another side, it launched a project of competing in direct with Lazard in North America, where historically it had failed to get embedded: it opened offices in New York, Washington, Los Angeles and Chicago, and also in Toronto, with teams of senior bankers, with the intent to penetrate into the huge local M&A market. The wave of globalization has been translated in the number of countries where both banks are present in 2016: 44 for Rothschild (with 3,300 employees and managers) and 27 for Lazard (with 2,610 employees).

D. The issue of competitiveness

Such houses are enduring acute competition and their frailty lies with the loss of financial positions in case of strong offensives from rivals,[16] the departure of brilliant managers (to competitors, for their own boutique or to head companies). Acute capital of talent is ever at stake. Lazard had to leave for example the trio of leaders in M&As in France between 2006 and 2011. The duo B. Roger-M. Pigasse had to reinvent the portfolio of skills and connections of Lazard Paris; and that was the case in the area of financial advice to States. A risk lies with the very quality of managers as several of them are "invited" to join other banks – Pierre Tattevin, at Lazard since 1982 and associate in 1995, left in 2000 to join Rothschild US, then came back at Lazard in 2010, joined by François Kayat, at Credit Suisse First Boston since 1998 and then in 2006 managing director of Crédit agricole CIB (Calyon) and global head of M&A – State institutions – at the Élysée general secretary, for François Pérol (Rothschild in 2005–2007) by Nicolas Sarkozy, and Emmanuel Macron (at Rothschild in 2008–2012) by François Hollande, both coming from

---

[16] See: Olivier Pastré, *Les nouveaux piliers de la finance*, Paris, La Découverte, 1992.

Rothschild – and more frequently the leading team of big companies or investment funds.

This turnover might be balanced by the attractiveness of merchant houses, as they draw high civil servants who attended altogether the big administration and the cabinets of ministers and bring their *carnet d'adresses* (or box of contacts) throughout the State institutions or public and private business. Senior bankers coming out of ministerial cabinets or high administration permanently renew the staff, and then are initiated by partners or high managers into connected banking, along a legacy of immaterial capital. Even some kind of "stars" took up the torch in each house to become key advisors to big operations – like Grégoire Chertok, having completed about 150 deals in 25 years at Rothschild, Sébastien Proto and François Wat, at Rothschild – as a proof of the permanency of the legacy of finance, in the wake of their glorious predecessors of the end of the 20th century.

Relational banking is the very business culture of both banks, which explains rumours and facts about their (secretive or patent) influence on each market place, among the business communities, and at the heart of ministers in charge of economics and finance – which led to articles and books insisting on the hidden (but clear-cut) side of their life. On that field too, the legacy of finance is obvious!

"The big houses are prisoners of the type of relations which they have with the companies that can think of such operations of M&A; they are often confronted to conflicts of interests because, if they intervene, it is for the financing of the operations. At their scale, the commissions of M&A are small with regard to the activities of market banking. Another issue is the position of the individuals in a big structure that cannot bear too big disparities of remuneration between the good basic banker and the person in charge of M&A, whereas, in a small house, the shareholders have a low return on capital because the main part of the profits is suited to the partners.

About what involves the working mode, less organized into a rigid hierarchy, each senior banker has his customers like in a law firm. As it is a job much commercial, it is necessary to entice the appetite of associates, who wish to overtake a mere monthly income. It is necessary for them to create operations, to find out the customer, to seduce him, to convince him individually, before the basic work made by one equip. There is a relation between the commercial success and the remuneration of the banker, which is far higher than in the big organizations.

In a little house bank, a person is in charge in particular, the relation and the responsibility are identified. Bruno Roger made a fortune at Lazard that he would never have reached in a big bank, as well as François Henrot, who left the Paribas finance company for Rothschild. It is the difference between the ready-to-wear clothing, even high-end, and the custom-made product; M&A are always of the ready-to-wear clothing. On the big amounts, the big banks involve their balance sheet, for all transactions of financing and market. Conversely, because the *Haute Banque* houses were created by families, which have for characteristic ceilings in their assets, they ever hated the idea to lose them by playing risks."[17]

2. A key target: Skills and competitiveness about mergers & acquisitions

The "legacy of finance" results before all into an endless renewal and extension of the portfolio of skills in merchant banking, through a basic activity which gathered momentum from the 1950s to 1970s and reached a broad extension from the 1990s to 2000s, when capitalism had to be restructured to face competition – from French, European or American companies, along the steps of the development of "open economies." Rothschild and Lazard embodied such a move towards advising banking beyond underwriting; but they have to face harsh competition from the American offshoots in Paris or London.

The financial battle that led two French pharmaceutical companies to struggle one another was for instance revealing on that field: Merrill Lynch-Paris and BNP Paribas advised the bidder Sanofi – whilst its main capital-holder Total relied on HSBC France (ex Crédit commercial de France, CCF) – whereas the defender Aventis was helped by Rothschild, but also by Goldman Sachs and Morgan Stanley. All in all: three teams from American banks (and one British-owned) versus one sole on the side of the Paris merchant houses club, even if brilliant French brains

17 Interview with an investment banker, April 2017.

were active within American M&A teams, like Patrick Ponsolle by Morgan Stanley or Marc Pandraud by Merrill Lynch.[18]

A. Mergers & acquisitions profiting to Rothschild and Lazard

The "financialization" of worldwide economy,[19] the convergence of national economies within the unified European market, the upsurge of internationalized investment funds,[20] the globalization process and its effects on the competitiveness of firms[21] – having to grow through external growth and to focus on key activities – the amalgamation trend fuelled by French tycoon businessmen[22] (Vincent Bolloré, Bernard Arnault, the Pinault father and son, etc.) – and a new wave of extension of American companies in Europe explained a rush to mergers & acquisitions (M&A).[23] They have been justified in the name of industrial

---

[18] Elsa Conesa, "De belles perspectives pour les banques d'affaires," *Les Échos*, January 27, 2004. Sanofi-Aventis became then the first pharmaceutical firm in Europe and the third worldwide.

[19] François Morin & Claude Dupuy (eds.), *Le cœur financier européen*, Paris, Économica, 1993. François Morin, *La grande rupture*, Paris, La Découverte, 2007.

[20] *Cf.* Dominique Plihon & Jean-Pierre Ponssard (eds.), *La montée en puissance des fonds d'investissements*, Paris, La Documentation française, 2002. Claude Dupuy & Stéphanie Lavigne (eds.), *Géographies de la finance mondialisée*, Paris, La Documentation française, 2009. Med Kechidi, "Croissance externe et investisseurs institutionnels internationaux," *Sciences de la société*, October 2001, no. 54, p. 111–134.

[21] See: "Les nouveaux enjeux de la compétitivité," introduction to: Bertrand Bellon & Jean-Marie Chevalier (dir.), *L'industrie en France*, Paris, Flammarion, 1983. Élie Cohen & Michel Bauer, *Les grandes manœuvres industrielles*, Paris, Belfond, 1985. Institut d'histoire de l'industrie, *L'industrie française face à l'ouverture internationale*, Paris, Économica, 1991.

[22] Michel Villette & Catherine Vuillermot, *Portrait de l'homme d'affaires en prédateur*, Paris, La Découverte, 2005. Michel Villette & Catherine Vuillermot, *From Predators to Icons. Exposing the Myth of the Business Hero*, Cornell University Press, 2009. Pierre-Angel Gay & Caroline Monnot, *François Pinault milliardaire, ou les secrets d'une incroyable fortune*, Paris, Belfond, 1999. Nathalie Raulin & Renaud Lecadre, *Vincent Bolloré, enquête sur un capitalisme au-dessus de tout soupçon*, Paris, Denoël, 2000. Airy Routier, *L'ange exterminateur, la vraie vie de Bernard Arnault*, Paris, Albin Michel, 2003. Michel Pinçon & Monique Pinçon-Charlot, *Nouveaux patrons, nouvelles dynasties*, Paris, Calmann-Lévy, 1999.

[23] Baudouin Prot & Michel de Rosen, *Le retour du capital. Les fusions-acquisitions en France et dans le monde*, Paris, Odile Jacob, 1990.

and services restructurings and "strategies," sometimes through financial battles on the Stock Exchange.[24]

The business of merchant banking, in a restrictive and precise way, as that of speciality in advice and conduct of the mergers and acquisitions, acquired a broad scale at the demand of offensive or defensive firms. A symbol of the acuteness of the Lazard and Rothschild teams has been delivered at the start of 2021: When the Canadian commercial group Couche Tard declared its intent to propose the purchase of the second French distribution group, Carrefour, it chose an *associé-gérant* at Rothschild, Cyril de Montmarin – who had already been the advisor of the present CEO of Carrefour, Alexandre Bompard, when that latter organized the merger of FNAC and Darty in 2016; in the meanwhile, Carrefour had rather to be advised by Lazard.[25]

Investment banking had to reinvent itself – whereas its market banking divisions prospered.[26] Sure the specialized departments of classical universal banks remained competitive rivals, all the more that BNP acquired the French investment bank Paribas in 2000 and the Belgian Fortis in 2009, and Crédit agricole purchased the investment bank Indosuez[27] in 1996 and Crédit lyonnais in 2003, and aggregated their teams into CACIB (Crédit Agricole Corporate & Investment Bank). But offensives by US banks were still much harder to resist, as they set up dynamic teams in London, Paris, etc. Goldman Sachs, Merrill Lynch and Morgan Stanley became embedded there, and, on second level, the corporate and investment banking divisions of universal banks could also take part to the game (Citicorp, Bancamerica, Barclays Capital, HSBC, which has integrated the teams of CCF).

This whole bunch of bankers practice cross-selling proposals, with loans to companies committed in M&A operations, in front of

---

24 See: Hubert Bonin & Bertrand Blancheton (eds.), *Crises et batailles boursières aux XXe et XXIe siècles*, Geneva, Droz, 2017.

25 Ivan Letessier & Marie Bartnik, "Malgré le veto de Le Maire, Carrefour et Couche-Tard continuent de négocier un projet de mariage", *Le Figaro*, January 14, 2021.

26 "From history to present: Investment banking at stake," chapter 15, in Hubert Bonin & Carlo Brambilla (eds.), *Investment Banking History. National and Comparative Issues (19th-21st Centuries)*, "Euroclio. Studies and Documents," Brussels, Peter Lang, 2014, p. 471–507.

27 Hubert Bonin, *Indosuez. L'autre grande banque d'affaires (1975–1987)*, Paris, Économica, 1987.

"non-lending banks" like the merchant banks. M&A often seem to lack profitability or to provide meagre commissions (from dozens to hundred million euros/dollars) in front of margins reached for the IPOs – needing large and intense networks for the brokerage process – or loans. As a counterpart, merchant bankers can often bet on the restrictions put on M&A projects by chief financial officers at big banks because of this issue of profits, and they can therefore jump over them without hesitations, whilst mobilising their advising talent.

B. *Sharpening skills in financial advice*

Specialized merchant banks had then to counterattack. They renewed and extended their teams. "Stars" of M&A, relieved by teams of "junior managers," mobilized their capital of skills understanding financial engineering, osmosis between stock exchange transactions and offer of the loans allowing to finance them, business law, optimal management of a "address book," useful for the positive connections and for the fight against the asymmetry of information.

The 1980s marked maybe a new peak of Lazard: "The characteristic of the French market is its concentration around a traditionally dominant actor, the house Lazard. In 1988 it realized 43 deals for a 55.7 billion FRF total, among which many of the big affairs (Seagram/Martell, Sweat/SGB, LVMH/Arnault/Guinness). Its market share is more of double of that of his closest competitor, Indosuez (25,9 billion FRF), quadruples of CCF, Paribas, Société générale, Crédit lyonnais (11–13 billion FRF)."[28] Such a capacity of resistance explains the ability to play on the ground of bigwigs, either French, European or American ones (see Tab. 1).

[28] Olivier Costa de Beauregard & Jean-Pierre Denis, « Une vitalité méconnue », in Baudoin Prot & Michel de Rosen (eds.), *Le retour du capital. Les fusions-acquisitions en France et dans le monde*, Paris, Odile Jacob, 1990, p. 204.

Tab. 1. The leading investment banks on the French market for M&A operations (total of operations in value) in 1989–2003

1989	Average 1991–1995	1996	2003
Lazard frères	Lazard frères	Lazard frères	Goldman Sachs
Paribas	BNP	Banexi (BNP)	Rothschild et Cie
SG Warburg (USA/UK)	Goldman Sachs	Goldman Sachs	Morgan Stanley
Goldman Sachs (USA)	Crédit lyonnais	Paribas	JP Morgan
Morgan Stanley (USA)	Paribas	Rothschild et Cie	Lazard (France/ USA)
Crédit lyonnais	Société générale	Morgan Stanley	Citigroup (USA)
CCF	Rothschild et Cie (France)	Société générale	Crédit agricole-Crédit lyonnais
Financière Indosuez	SBC Warburg	JP Morgan	Société générale
Banexi (Bnp)	JP Morgan	Deutsche Bank Morgan Grenfell	BNP Paribas
Salomon Brothers (USA)	Morgan Stanley	Clinvest (Crédit lyonnais)	Deutsche Bank
Baring Brothers	Lehman Brothers (USA)		Merrill Lynch (USA)
JP Morgan (USA)	CCF		UBS (Switzerland)
Société générale	ING Barings		
RN Clive Worms & Cie	Crédit Suisse First Boston		
Bankers Trust (USA)	Deutsche Bank Morgan Grenfell (Germany and UK)		

Source: Journal *Fusions & acquisitions*
Source: *Capital Finance*; operations closed in 2003, taking into account the value of firms, in proportion to the transactions, except internal restructurings.

C. Portfolios of skills and connections as recent advantage edges: The case of Lazard

Rich with about two dozen *associés-gérants* (led by Mathieu Pigasse), Lazard Paris intervenes for the benefit of his customers on a wide range of strategic and financial questions. The advice in M&A covers any operation of external growth or disinvestment. It also advises on other structuring operations such as recapitalizations, spin-offs or splits. It brings stuff to ailing firms and supplies them restructuring plans – and it was the case during the big operations of restructuring caused by the financial crisis of 2007–2008. It supplies matter on the questions of structure of capital and levying of capital, in particular about financing transactions on highly rated markets or unquoted. Relationship management plays a leverage role in corporate finance and debt advisory services – and this is one key advantage edge for merchant houses – far from transaction banking, market activities, forex and risk management about derivatives. Less permanent funds are required, and more agility is available as the chain of decisions is lighter because of the smaller risks to be confronted with.

Battles on the stock-exchange contribute to check the talents of banking advisors. That was the case first when rivals attempted to take the control of Compagnie de Suez, its financial assets and Indosuez bank in 1994–1995; BNP dreamed of "*très grande financière*" uniting BNP, Suez and insurer UAP whereas Crédit agricole intended to cement its recent leadership on the Paris marketplace. Lazard was chosen by BNP to design financial tricks to get the control over Suez without launching a public bid, and it almost succeeded with a big minority of the votes at the general assembly of Suez.[29] Later on, in 1996, Lazard was the adviser to BNP in front of Goldman Sachs, that of Crédit agricole when both banks struggled to convince Suez to choose each of them for the sale of Indosuez. Last, during the fight between BNP and Société générale for the control over Paribas in 1999–2000, Rothschild (François Henrot) was on the side of Paribas and Lazard on the side of BNP (with Goldman-Sachs) as they competed to conceive attractive projects for stake- and shareholders.

D. The case of Rothschild

The revolution in Rothschild's life has been its drift from French and European deals to globalized ones, all the more because M&A operations followed the same process: recent operations epitomize such a move (Tab. 2). Documents in institutional communication prove the globalized stature of Rothschild: Rothschild in the Middle East, Rothschild in Japan. They detail the deals concluded in such areas and internationally.[30]

---

[29] See: Lucien Douroux, *Un voyage inattendu. De mon village auvergnat à la tête du Crédit agricole*, Paris, Cherche Midi, 2016, p. 259–262.

[30] Documents available at the Rothschild headquarters in London. We thank head archivist Melanie Aspey to have introduced us thereinto.

Tab. 2. Examples of recent operations in M&A

	Involving Rothschild	Involving Lazard
2005	Advice for the merger of both investment banks of Caisses d'épargne and Banques populaires into Natixis	
2014	Advisors to Publicis for the (failed) merger with Omnicom, with the boutique Moelis on the side of the US firm	
	Merger of Lafarge and Holcim (Switzerland)	
2015	Acquisition of Alstom Energy by GE	
	Acquisition of Xerox ITO (US) by Atos (France)	
	Sale of Verallia by Saint-Gobain	
2015–2016	BG Group to be purchased by Royal Dutch Shell	
2016	Merger of Technip and FMC (with Goldman Sachs), FMC being supported by Société générale and Evercore	BAT purchasing Reynolds (tobacco, US)
	Acquisition of Fairmont Raffles (US) by Accor	Tyco merger with Johnson Controls (US)
	Sale by Casino of its Thai affiliate	Acquisition of WhiteVawe (US) by Danone
	Merger between Fnac and Darty	SoftBank Group (Japan) purchase of ARM Holdings (US)
		Deutsche Börse intending to amalgam with London Stock Exchange
2017	Volvo Trucks ceding Renault Trucks Défense	Mandate to prepare the spin-off of Body Shop from L'Oréal
	Olivier Pécoux, CEO of Rothschild & Co (and a member of the board of Essilor), main advisor for the purchase of Luxottica by Essilor	

Continued

Tab. 2. Continued

	Involving Rothschild	Involving Lazard
	François Henrot advisor of Safran for the financial and technical negotiations with Zodiac	Zodiac being advised by Lazard
	Advisor of Safran for the sale of Morpho (digital security) to Oberthur-Advent (advised by Lazard)	
	Advisor of the investment fund PAI for the sale of three assets for a value of 2 billion €	
		Advisor for the Thales bid on Gemalto, with Messier Maris & Associés and Société générale – Gemalto advised by Deutsche Bank and JP Morgan
	Purchase by Unibail-Rodamco (property asset management) of Westfield (commercial malls)	

Source: journals; *Rothschild in France. Global Financial Advisory*, Rothschild documentary office, London.

E. From the legacy to the future of finance: The upsurge of boutiques

Beyond both leaders, the fad for *boutiques* gathered momentum from the 2000s, mainly in asset and wealth management (Carmignac, Oddo, etc.), but also in merchant banking.[31] Strong characters, rich with *carnets d'adresses*, experience, and capital of reputation, seized on the opportunities to mix "coaching" of CEOs about their business model and financial advice, in the name of confidentiality and conceptual agility. Several boutiques asserted themselves as actors of the Paris market-place: Messier (led by Jean-Marie Messier), Philippe Villin (along the name of its boss), Aforge Finance, Toulouse & Associés (Jean-Baptiste Toulouse, moving from Rothschild), Financière de Courcelles, Leonardo (Michel Cicurel, for a while), Bucéphale Finance (2004), etc., bet on the intimacy thus

---

[31] See: Mélanie Delattre, "Les petites boutiques de la haute finance," *Le Point*, June 15, 2006, p. 76–80.

forged, the permanency of their little teams, and their added value, there too against the profile of big banks. A revealing case in the US might be that of Centerview: it was set up in 2006 by Blair Effron, who had worked by Dillon-Read then UBS; and it emerged as a very specialist of M&A and advice boutique, even opening an offset in Paris in 2020, where it welcomed as partner Mathieu Pigasse and other experimented investment bankers.[32]

Largillière Finance

« Fondée en 2005, par Paul Bougnoux et Tanguy Mantelin, Largillière Finance est une société indépendante de conseil en fusions-acquisitions basée à Paris, Bruxelles et Genève. Nous conseillons nos clients sur leurs opérations de cessions et d'acquisitions de sociétés, de levées de fonds, en ingénierie financière et en tant que conseil stratégique. Nos clients sont les dirigeants d'ETI, de PME et leurs actionnaires. Nous intervenons en France et à l'international à travers nos bureaux et le réseau international i-Deal-Net dont nous sommes l'un des fondateurs. L'équipe Largillière Finance est constituée d'une vingtaine de professionnels. Elle est renforcée par un réseau de seniors advisors, experts de haut niveau, qui apportent compétences techniques et sectorielles. Nos équipes travaillent ensemble grâce à une méthodologie unique basée sur le travail collaboratif, l'échange d'informations et le partage de la connaissance. Nous conseillons les dirigeants d'entreprises et les actionnaires dans leurs stratégies de cession ou de croissance externe: cession, acquisition, LBO, alliance stratégique, joint-venture, etc. Nous accompagnons nos clients dans leur développement auprès des investisseurs et des partenaires financiers adaptés pour leurs projets de financement: fonds propres, quasi-fonds propres, dette senior, obligations convertibles, etc. »

But bigwigs themselves were convinced to decentralize their modus operandi and to reignite the spirit and practice of the *Haute Banque*. Foreign

32 Thibault Madelin & François Vidal, "Le grand entretien: Blair Effron," *Les Échos*, May 21, 2021. Bruna Biasini, "Centerview Partners, la banque qui veut secouer la place de Paris," *Journal du dimanche*, January 11, 2021.

banks thus opened subsidiaries looking as merchant banking houses: DC Advisory by Daiwa, Aelios Finance within the Oaklins franchise in 2016, or Raymond James Financial, etc. Last, big leading banks used to work as partners to *Haute Banque* houses like Rothschild or Lazard in recent M&A operations, even from London for Zaoui & Co – which joined Rothschild as advisors for the merger between Lafarge and Holcim in 2014 – from Paris or New York (Evercore, Moelis, etc.).

No immediate "legacy of finance" can be found there, of course, but a new stage of the history of investment banking. The ex-high civil servant and chairman of Vivendi Jean-Marie Messier launched his *boutique* in 2003 (Messier, Maris & Associés since 2010, when Erik Maris left Lazard to join him) and succeeded in conquering space for manœuvre since then.[33] A showcase was the role played by Bucéphale Finance to advice Banques populaires and Caisse d'épargne to join their investment banks and set up Natixis in 2006, whereas Lazard was put aside before joining the team as sub-partner.

F. Resisting the grip of bigwigs

Despite these portfolios of skills, connections, and positions, each merchant house has to endure the rhythm of business deals, which explains that rankings often change from one year to the following one (Tabs. 3 and 4); and they depend on the rhythm of M&A in each business area along the volatility of sectors.[34] Far from the dimension reached by Goldman Sachs, ranked first by Thomson-Reuters with one third of the world market with advices to operations amounting to 1,800 billion $ in 2016, both Rothschild and Lazard remain stable stake-holders of the M&A market, even if the first one might seem lacking a worldwide network, conversely with Lazard, also deeply embedded in the US.

---

33 Valérie de Senneville, "Le come-back de Jean-Marie Messier," *Les Échos*, November 4, 2011, p. 10. Clément Lacombe, "La deuxième vie de Jean-Marie Messier. Renaissance. L'ancien banquier est devenu un banquier d'affaires à succès," *Le Point*, December 17, 2015, no. 2258–2259, p. 97–105.

34 See: "The 2016 M&A Report. Masters of Corporate Folio," *BCG-Perspectives*, August 30, 2016.

Tab. 3. The leading banks on the worldwide M&A market in 2012

	2011	2012	Volume of transaction in 2012 (billons dollars)
Goldman Sachs	1	1	394.6
JP Morgan	2	2	348.2
Morgan Stanley	4	3	334.2
Deutsche Bank	8	4	269.4
Barclays	7	5	264.6
Crédit Suisse	3	6	263.8
Citi	6	7	260.8
Bank of America-Merrill Lynch	5	8	220.5
Rothschild	11	9	145
Lazard	10	10	122.4

Source: Dealogic; *Les Échos*, September 26, 2012.

The key word is: competition. In front of "big wigs," *Haute Banque* houses have to endlessly foster new skills and spirit into the game. When the electronics Atos group tried to bid on Gemalto at the very end of 2017, JP Morgan and Deutsche Bank ran to advise that latter before Société générale, Lazard and Messier-Maris were recruited by Thales to conceive a counter-bid, which will be achieved in 2018.[35] Such harsh confrontations are being frequent on the technology markets, where start-ups or "unicorns" are selling themselves to strong actors of the third industrial revolution, which need to close innovation gaps.

"High-tech deals represented almost 30 % of total $2.7 trillion of completed transactions in 2016 … Competition increases for large-scale, must-have assets as more traditional buyers, backed by substantial M&A bankrolls, seek technological innovations," generating "bidding wars."[36] "Internal M&A teams tend to specialize more in industry segments and technologies that are close to home. Sourcing tech targets requires wider search parameters and expertise … More agile deal execution [demands] shorter due diligence time frames,"[37] but bankers have to rely more and more on internal "deal teams" rich in senior advisors.

35 Sandrine Cassini, Isabelle Chaperon & Guy Dutheil, "Les coulisses de la bataille Thales-Atos pour Gemalto," *Le Monde. Économie & entreprises*, December 19, 2017, p. 7.

36 See: BCG-Boston Consulting Group, *The 2017 M&A Report. The Technology Takeover*, September 2017.

37 *Ibidem.*

Tab. 4. Ranking of advisory banking contributions to M&A in 2015–2016 (announced deals in billions dollars)

Ranking in Europe in 2016		Ranking in France in 2016		Ranking in France en 2015
Goldman Sachs	455.3	63.4	Rothschild	4th
Morgan-Stanley	338.2	45.8	Lazard	10th
JP Morgan	266	44.8	Goldman Sachs	6th
Lazard	234.6	39.8	Crédit agricole Investment Banking	14th
BofA-Merrill Lynch	215.9	37.1	Morgan Stanley	2d
UBS	209	30.2	Crédit suisse	11th
Deutsche Bank	182.2	27.9	Citi	7th
Barclays	123.2	26.1	BofA-Merrill Lynch	1st
		24.1	BNP Paribas	3th
		20.5	Société générale	5th

Source: Anne Drif, "Les fusions-acquisitions reculent dans le monde sur fond d'incertitudes politiques," *Les Échos*, January 2, 2017, p. 24–25.

In 2016, Rothschild completed 123 M&A operations, with a value of 63.3 billion €, whilst Lazard tackled 61 operations with a value of 45.8 billion: they keep therefore their historical position as key stake-holders of the Paris market-place. In 2017 Rothschild dominated Lazard on the M&A rankings, with an amount of $122 billion of announced operations, against 71 billion. Both resisted to the offensive by BNP Paribas and Goldman Sachs.[38]

But both teams were convinced to avoid rushing for M&A deals that could reveal disappointing afterwards, as it had been the case during each booming cycle from the 1980s across the Atlantic, because of extra-costs and risks of execution, at times when so many investment bankers delivered demanding advice to ample external growth. Lessons have been drawn from the 2001 to 2003 and 2007 to 2009 crisis, and it seems that times have come to refocus, cutting into grease, defining key activities, and investment bankers from the smaller houses are playing an eminent role in such a rehearsal of strategies, despite competition from

38 Thomson Reuters, January 2018.

the business units at universal banks, themselves rich with high-range managers, advisors, and analysts.

The 2020–2021 battle between the two French leaders of utilities (management of water and waste) Veolia and Suez was revealing of the balance between the investment banking units of big banks and surviving *Haute Banque* houses. The three involved companies – as Engie had just sold its 32 % stake in Suez to Veolia through a spin-off operation – recruited a large array of bankers as advisors, with even the boutique of Jean-Marie Messier (Tab. 5).[39]

Tab. 5. Investment bankers involved in the Veolia-Suez battle in 2020–2021

***Haute Banque* houses**	**Big foreign banks**	**Big French banks**	**Boutiques**
Perella-Weinberg Partners Lazard Rothschild	Citi HSBC Morgan Stanley Bank of America Merrill Lynch Credit Suisse Goldman Sachs JP Morgan Barclays	Crédit agricole BNP Paribas	Messier (with a share of 60 % by Mediobanca since 2019)

G. The ever active spirit of Haute Banque

The challenge for Lazard and Rothschild – and the *boutiques* – is to insufflate more fluid sense of what is within a strict professional grip of knowledge about market areas and productive sectors, what lays with a comprehensive restructuring of incumbent firms to resist incoming forces with speed and agility, essential to competitiveness. One understands finally how far advising bankers have to extend their mixed analysis and proposals: geo-economics, business strategies, financial perspectives for external resources (loans, stocks), cross-border and even globalized

[39] Mathieu Pechberty, “Les banques d’affaires se ruent sur l’offre de Veolia sur Suez,” *BFM Business*, September 9, 2020. Robert Lafont, “Redevenu seul maître à bord de sa banque d’affaires, Jean-Marie Messier négocie le deal du siècle : la reprise de Suez par Veolia,” *BFM Business*, November 2, 2020.

schemes. The very quality of light banks could be the breaking up of entrenched specialized departments often predominating at big banks.

"We evaluate potential targets or merger partners as well as financial and strategic alternatives. We advise on strategy, timing, structure, financing, pricing, and we assist in negotiating and closing transactions. In addition, we act as a dealer-manager in tender or exchange offers."[40] Perhaps should we value a difference in business cultures in practices that could insufflate competitiveness on the part of *Haute Banque* houses: when deals were to be designed, "the Americans came with consultants' kits, specialized with portfolios of fifty pages, and imposed a culture of seller of financial products. The historic English culture disappeared, the one according to which, when you visit a big specialist, we look for a diagnosis and a treatment, without making big reports."[41]

"The culture of the American merchant bank leaves an extreme specialization of the persons in charge by business sector or by job. All the jobs which make the business bankers and all the domains of the economic are specialized. The industrialization of this business was imperative (industrial banking). These banks have so full of conflicts of interests, in spite of the official compartmentalization within the firm. And they have only hyper-specialists; yet companies are sometimes organized in a vertical way, with one or two decision-makers in some, who do not want to work with a team of several specialists. That's what created the need for independent banks, with a speaking banker with several hats. We correspond to the fact that number of bosses expect from the banker for advice; in the US the business law firms hold from now on this role; in France this business still exists, and it is the heart of the business of Rothschild and Lazard."[42]

From the turn of the century, "we protected a culture and especially a French "technicality," as Rohatyn had identified it. It is necessary to know enough right, accounting and tax system, without being locked into your reflections by an army of jurists, accountants and tax experts who wish to impose their constraints. The business bankers became very expert in these three specialties, resting on good business lawyers, firms

---

40 Lazard institutional communication, 2017.

41 Interview with an investment banker at Rothschild, April 2017.

42 *Ibidem*.

of audit and on tax consultants, with whom the banker works. This financial engineering constitutes a real French talent."[43]

3. *Haute Banque* houses active on the underwriting market

Rothschild and Lazard had been historically much active on the underwriting market, as lead or co-lead advisors or mere members of syndicates, and the legacy of finance did cross the recent decades. Sure they cannot compete with big internationalized banks on the underwriting market where competition has been intensified; and the effects of the domination of investment banking by the American banks are to be countered.[44] But they have entertained and renewed their heritage on that segment, to conquer some crumbs of big deal, for States or companies. The more they advise States, for example, the more they can accede to market shares in the wake of their immaterial role. "We advise clients on a broad range of strategic and tactical issues, including capital structure optimization, capital allocation, equity and debt market positioning and issuance, and investor communications strategies."[45]

This explains that, far behind bigwigs, they still keep some ranking on the investment banking market (Tab. 6), which put together M&A, equity, bonds and syndicated loans into a single amount. French banks are struggling against US or Europe (Deutsche Bank, Barclays) leaders; and the bigwigs might seem to choke *Haute Banque* houses; but a look at the actual percentages show that only a few points separate them, and that they even compete with the subsidiary of Banques populaires-Caisses d'épargne, Natixis.

43 *Ibidem.*

44 See: "The United States dominates global investment banking: Does it matter for Europe?," *Bruegel Policy Contribution*, March 2016.

45 Lazard institutional communication, 2017.

Tab. 6. Rankings along market share in overall investment banking (11-year average from 2005 to 2015)

	2005	2006	2007	2008	2009	2010	2011	2012	2013	2014	2015
Rothschild	1.7	1.1	1.3	1.3	0.5	0.7	0.9	1	0.7	0.6	1
Lazard	0.7	0.6	0.5	0.8	0.8	0.9	0.8	0.7	0.5	0.8	0.9
BNP Paribas	5.4	5	5.2	5.5	5.5	5	5.7	4.5	5.2	4.7	4.4
Société générale	3.5	3.1	2.6	2.7	3.3	3	3.4	2.5	2.8	2.8	2.6
CACIB (Crédit agricole)	3.5	2.7	2.4	3	2.7	2.6	3.2	2.6	2.4	2.7	2.5
Natixis	1.5	1.5	1.1	1.1	1.2	1.5	1.8	1.6	1.4	1.6	1.4
JP Morgan	6.5	7	6.4	8.5	8.7	7.9	6.8	7.9	7.3	7.5	7.6

Source: "Global investment banking review, full year 2015," Thomson-Reuters Deals Business Intelligence, New York, 2016; "The United States dominates global investment banking: Does it matter for Europe?," *Bruegel Policy Contribution*, March 2016.

Complementarities between M&A and underwriting may appear, and the houses may be actors of the group of banks helping the purchaser of a company to finance its deal, either through a M&A operation or as a result of spin-off. Debt advice was for instance supplied by Rothschild to FNAC when it bought Darty in 2016; and it was also the adviser on the IPO by Europcar in 2015, when sold by Eurazeo, or when Verallia was purchased by Apollo Global Management (2015). A landmark operation was the contribution to the capital increase by PSA Peugeot-Citroën in 2014, with the renewal of a syndicated revolving credit facility and services to the programme of cooperation between PSA and the Chinese Dongfeng Motor Cy. A team advised the transit management Necotrans (in Africa) to extend its capital in 2016.

The booklet *Leading in Financial Advice, Worldwide* (2016) analyses the whole range of deals concluded on a world scale by Rothschild as a "global financial advisory" house. "With approximately 900 advisers in 40 countries around the world, our scale, reach, intellectual capital and local knowledge enable us to develop relationships and deliver effective solutions to our clients, wherever their business takes them."

Rothschild's classical field have been extended broadly in equity advisory and capital raisings, and also as an intermediary between institutions and the book-running banks to get from them the best deals – and the same about private firms. This can explain that Rothschild was the "adviser on over 300 IPOs, secondary offerings, block trades, spin-offs and convertible bonds since 2010, totalling US$ 410 billion." The field of advice to States and public institutions – like the sovereign funds of the Middle East – has been reignited from the turn of the century, and a pioneering lady partner asserted herself with Anne-Laure Kiechel, the head of the department.

Lazard, from its Parisian office, accompanied governments in their financial projects: privatizations, restructurings of debt, sovereign notation; that was the case for cases concerning Greece, Argentina (100b $), Ecuador, Iraq, Ivory Coast or Egypt. In 2010–2012, it was a banker-advice of the Greek government, about the restructuring of the Greek private debt (200b €) and the process of banking restructuring, and Rothschild took part to this reorganization of the public debt holder PDMA too. In 2015 Lazard was in charge of supporting this country about the national debt and about the management of the fiscal policy. A team of about twenty "economist bankers" is active on that field from Paris, under the guidance of M. Pigasse. An advantage edge might be the specialization in advice: "When was created the job of advice to the governments, to exercise this job, we should be independent; we cannot lend to the governments and restructure their debt, and on the other hand negotiate on this debt; there would be conflict of interests."[46]

4. Business models and strategies at stake

Beyond the core M&A activity, both Rothschild and Lazard defined a few other strategic developments, first because of complementarities between the brokerage of securities issued for the account of firms and states, but second mainly as a legacy of their history in the valuation of assets for the account of their customers, being institutions (asset management), or individuals (wealth management). The heritage of their history is obvious throughout these paths, but innovative processes had to be followed to resist specialized companies or universal banks.

Even if Rothschild took 20 % of a broker Smith New Court, both houses decided to stay out of "primary finance" and "market banking," conversely with Goldman Sachs, notably. The strategic choice was clear-cut at Rothschild, conversely with Lazard; there, harsh arguments occurred at the turn of the century, with even some kind of revolt in New York, which had to be appeased by M. David-Weill, to stick to the

[46] Interview with an investment banker at Rothschild, April 2017

historical business fields and avoid the involvement in risks demanding deep permanent funds. Such respect of "the legacy of finance" could contribute to explain that Lazard and Rothschild escaped the booming risks of the 2000s and the collapse of 2007–2008 (in opposition with Merrill-Lynch, Bear Stearns or others).

A. Haute Banque houses as rescuers of capitalism?

From the M&A market and on the verge of underwriting and debt-management activities, *Haute Banque* houses are more and more following the trend to advice States and companies when they need to restructure their debt, balance sheet and portfolio of assets. Bankers try and re-dispatch parts of the activities of firms; they renegotiated the maturation, size and structure of public or private debts, in connection with big banks, the bearers of loans or parts of the capital. The more capitalism has to be restructured and companies to reconsider their portfolio of activities or even to be rescued, the more the houses can develop this strategic segment, obtain mandates, gain commissions. "The much less readable and complex operations of refinancing and restructuring are numerous. And if investment funds are less committed, the industrialists are relatively active, pushed by a logic of debt pay-down."[47]

"Restructuring operation revenue was $202 million for 2016, compared to $106 million in 2015. During and since 2016, we have been engaged in a broad range of highly visible and complex restructuring and debt advisory assignments, including publicly announces roles for Alitalia,"[48] etc. "Lazard specializes in advising on out-of-court restructurings and recapitalizations. We have engineered many landmark transactions with favourable outcomes for our clients. We negotiate with creditors on behalf of our clients, especially in cases of financial stress or distress. We advise on and structure a wide variety of transactions, including tender and exchange offers, rescue financing or recapitalizations, 'amend and extend' amendments, as well as pre-packaged bankruptcies."[49]

---

47 Richard Thil, associé-gérant at Rothschild, *Les Échos*, September 21, 2012.

48 *Lazard Ltd reports full-year and fourth quarter 2016 results*, p. 3.

49 Lazard institutional communication, 2017.

Tab. 7. Recent examples of rescuing merchant banking by Rothschild and Lazard

2016	Attempts to rescue the oil services firm Bourbon and to renegociate its huge debt (in front of BNP Paribas)
2017	Mandate for the sale of the assets of failed Financière Turenne Lafayette (food industry)
	Mandate to find out a purchaser for the failing Flo group (restaurants)
	Lazard intervened for instance to the support of crippled Westinghouse in the US in to restructure its balance sheet and assets
	And of the weakened oil-related French firm CGG (with Morgan Stanley, Rothschild representing the holders of debt).

B. Developing asset management

Independent investment banks cannot of course compete with the giants in asset management, which grapple with several hundred billions euros – like Amundi (Crédit Agricole), Axa Investment Management, BNP Paribas Asset Management, or BlackRock (with more than three trillion \$). Anyway, tackling such issues can appear as a complement to their range of advices supplied to their intimate customers, or open larger doors to entice them to taste the other pieces of skills.

For instance, the activity of asset management of Lazard supplies management services on all the classes of assets about shares, rates, diversified, alternative products to institutional clients, companies, pension funds, foundations, insurance companies, banks, and to individual customers financial intermediaries and private customers worldwide. The aim is to produce the best yields fitted to the risk and to supply personalized solutions of investment. Today, about eight managers supervise Lazard Frères Gestion, strong with only about twenty billion €, but the whole group grappled with assets of about 198 billion € in 2016, versus 64 billion at Rothschild in 2016 (50.2 in 2015).

On that field, two Rothschild houses are competing, because the historical Rothschild of Paris has been challenged by the Edmond de Rothschild group. It had been set up in 1959 in Geneva and then disposed of a branch in Paris. Now headed by his stepdaughter Ariane de Rothschild, its strategy comprised a mix of asset and wealth management; despite its juniority the amount of the assets it manages today is four times bigger than those supervised by the senior Rothschild & Co house.

Through its 29 offices on three continents, the Swiss merchant bank Pictet entertains too the legacy of *Haute Banque*: "Observers of Swiss private banking say that the investment strength has been fuelled by Pictet's success as an asset manager. 'Wealth and asset management are two equally strong pillars of the bank – in terms of earning power and assets under management. There is no prioritization but rather a reciprocity between both business lines.'"[50]

C. Managing directly financial portfolios: True merchant banking

Investment bankers had ever entertained a tradition of supporting investment funds (or financial vehicles) in direct, to broaden their financial basis and get therefore complementary revenues, and moreover to help companies in their emergence, growth, and strategy, as such stakes could stabilize their shareholding. It might too foster new merchant banking opportunities as "captive markets" could be found out when financial operations were necessary. Power of influence and financial returns converged on quite different levels than banking itself.

Both Lazard and Rothschild managed such tools of investment. Lazard disposed historically of building companies (Rue impériale de Lyon, Immobilière marseillaise) and investment tools (Azeo, Eurafrance), to reinforce its influence within French capitalism and to help the equity of companies to evolve thanks to temporary stakes in property or equity. Anyway, Lazard reneged to such activity, conversely with Rothschild: it grouped its stakes into a financial holding, Eurazeo, in 2001, which became independent from Lazard in 2004 – even if M. David-Weill became then its chairman, starting a new financial life – merged with the previous affiliates, and followed its own path afterwards.[51]

On its side, PO and then Rothschild joined partners in investment-capital to hold stakes in a few dozen companies, generally speaking medium-sized ones (under turnovers of 100m €), because venture capital

50 "PWM/The Banker Private Banking Awards 2020," introduction to the special issue *Global Private Banking Awards 2020*, *The Banker*, November 2020, "Pictet. Best Private Bank in Europe and Switzerland," p. 8.

51 See [https://www.eurazeo.com/fr/la-societe/histoire/histoire/]. [https://www.lesechos.fr/11/10/2004/LesEchos/19262-161-ECH_eurazeo-reste-leste-par-l-heritage-lazard.htm#1LIfPkgpUmYQk13q.99].

has been rebirthed from 2003: in such a strategic move, Rothschild recalled the initiatives of the ancient house during the 19th century (in mining or else). But its size stays still very modest – along the guidance of Alexandre de Rothschild.

"Rothschild is a house of M&A even if it developed its know-how regarding financing to try to play too the intermediaries and to have a small part of commissions. She develops especially in the merchant banking, the manufacturing of investment funds intended for the wealthy customers willing to take risks in the non-highly rated, and she succeeds in it very well (private equity, secondary debt, funds of debts, according to the seniority of the debt). There is a layer of equity in the financing which are brought by the fund, another one is supplied by commercial banks, and, between both are situated funds subordinate to the classic debt, less to the risk than the equity, but riskier, thus better paid, what than we call the debt mezzanine. This one is replaced on the market according to the desires of the holders; and funds specialize in the repurchase in second hand of these titles of debt, with important commissions in the management of funds."[52]

5. A true tradition: Wealth management and private banking

History had forged solid strongholds around family and private banking houses about wealth management, earmarked to high-net-worth individuals with high levels of income or sizable assets, through services comprising discretionary asset management and brokerage, and dedicated advices about investments, taxes, and diversification. Such a tradition is still brilliant in Switzerland (Pictet, Mirabaud, Lombard Odier, Julius Baer, etc.), Austria and Germany, despite a few difficulties caused by bad management and moreover the necessity to respect recent regulations about transparency.

Competition gathered momentum when each big universal bank developed its strategy in that business, either through earmarked subsidiaries (NSM at ABN AMRO, 1819 at Caisses d'épargne, Indosuez Wealth Management at Crédit agricole, Banque du Luxembourg at Crédit mutuel, in

52 Interview with a senior investment banker, April 2017.

Luxembourg and Belgium,[53] etc.), or through specialized high range services (Société générale banque privée/Private Banking, rich with managed assets of 50 billion € in France in 2014, or BNP Paribas Wealth Management Banque privée). That latter "is a leading private bank worldwide and the leading private bank in the Eurozone. Present in three regions (Europe, Asia and the United States), it employs more than 6,800 professionals who accompany a clientele of private investors for the protection, growth and transmission of their assets, bringing long-term value to them, their families and society. As at 30 September 2020, the bank managed €380 billion in assets and was recently elected 'Best Private Bank' in Europe, North Asia, the West of the USA and the Middle East."[54]

The "ultra-rich" segments foster profitable trade; but Lazard and Rothschild can rely on their brand image (trust, tradition, durability, relative discretion), and moreover on the feelings of distinction.[55] Big banks head on this market in Europe in 2016, except Julius Baer (7th) and Pictet (9th), standing among the ten leaders considering the quality and range of services[56] – and neither Rothschild nor Lazard reach the 25 top list about managed assets.

Despite the huge dimension of such a market,[57] this competition induces merchant houses to reinvent their portfolio of skills, to assert differentiation, to insist on the immediate and long-term connections from earmarked customer managers in front of less stable and intimate officials by universal banks. The floor imposed to open and keep an

---

53 Bâtisseurs de mémoire, *Du CIAL à la Banque du Luxembourg, 1920–2020. Cent ans de banque à Luxembourg*, Luxembourg, édition en interne, 2020 [www.BDL.LU/100ANS].

54 [BNP Paribas Wealth Management présente ses 10 thèmes d'investissement pour 2021 – BNP Paribas (group.bnpparibas)].

55 Pierre Bourdieu, *La distinction. Critique sociale du jugement*, Paris, Éditions de Minuit, 1979. Monique Pinçon-Charlot & Michel Pinçon, *Sociologie de la bourgeoisie*, Paris, La Découverte, 2003, reedition, 2007. Monique Pinçon-Charlot & Michel Pinçon, *Grandes fortunes. Dynasties familiales et formes de richesse en France*, Paris, Payot, 2006. Monique Pinçon-Charlot & Michel Pinçon, *Voyage en grande bourgeoise. Journal d'enquête*, Paris, Puf, 2005.

56 *Euromoney Magazine*, February 2016. Annual ranking, Best private banks and wealth managers.

57 See: Brent Beardsley, Jorge Becerra, Federico Burgoni, Bruce Holley, Daniel Kessler, Federico Muxi, Matthias Naumann, Tjun Tang & Anna Zakrzewski, *Global Wealth 2014: Riding a Wave of Growth*, Bcg Perspectives, June 9, 2014.

account is far higher, which tends to jewellery management in favour of "ultra-riches," far from mere services to high-middle sized bourgeoisies. This is the very reason that well-paid advisers can be available and that the inquiries about the opportunities of a fine-tuned policy can be delivered to these well-off customers, all the more that they can belong to the stratus of managers of companies being already in touch with the bank. And the policy is to fight against "silos" and to propose personalized services to them about their personal assets management.

From the turn of the century, like any wealth management unit, Lazard – through its subsidiary Lazard Gestion, with Sophie de Nadaillac, *associée* since 2014 in charge of the development of private banking, and the two Rothschild banks imposed themselves velocity and agility along a transformational process to design the framework for their future, thanks to an intensified pace of adaptation. A key event occurred in 2016 when Rothschild France and the southern family bank Martin-Maurel decided to merge (with completion in the Spring 2017): it reinforced the stature in wealth management thanks to the input of faithful customership.[58]

Clients' centricity has been more and more critical as a way to make relationship more comprehensive, more durable, and more fruitful, both for the clients and the banks. A fresh mix of know-how and high-tech (cloud-based software, data mining, direct connection between the advisor and its customers) gathered momentum – whilst bridges with the asset management units were reinforced, mainly about the key role and prospects of "analysts" within the bank, often asserting themselves as consultants in the medias read by update people, for the sake of improving forecasting. One acute issue became "open architecture" *vs* "closed architecture." The first choice is to distribute all third-party products and not only proprietary products; the second one lies with proprietary products. But "pride" of solitude is no longer bearable and the three considered houses had to balance both architectures, depending on the demands of their customers, for the sake of agility.

The recent Covid-19 crisis did challenge the reactivity of wealth management teams: "This is a defining moment for private banks, whose relationship business of personal meetings has quickly transferred to a

58 Édouard Lederer & Ninon Renaud, "La banque Martin-Maurel s'apprête à fusionner avec Rothschild & C°," *Les Échos*, June 6, 2016.

series of screen interactions. Wealth advisers say cultural changes they expected to play out over years were implemented in a matter of weeks,"[59] which enhances the adaptability of the tool-box of these teams. "KBC Private Banking [in Belgium] has taken major steps to build a 'phygital' approach, whose main building block is an engine portfolio called *Iris*, which screens private banking portfolios daily, based on a risk-return factor algorithm, developed by the group's asset management arm. Alerting the private banker of any changes required to the client portfolio, it frees up their time, allowing a more customized advice."[60]

A second quality of *Haute Banque* practitioners has been also emphasized through the need to provide clients with an overall basket of advises. At UBS Wealth Management, "top management prides itself in having created a 'competitive advantage that's unmatched', through closer collaboration between different units. Its latest '3L' concept of liquidity, longevity and legacy has combined internal work on behavioural economics with research on clients' emotions and needs … 'The three Ls is not just a marketing slogan to us, it's the core of our philosophy', says Mr Khan [co-head of UBS Wealth Management], adding that the new concept helps 'frame conversations around what matters lost to our clients, and enables us to be their financial life partners."[61] But the CEO of BNP Paribas Banque privée France underlined anyway the legacy of Haute Banque bases: "Despite vast expenditure on digitalisation, this will remain very much a 'people business', based on 'trust and expertise'."[62] " 'Wealth management is inherently a people business', says Mr Busconi. 'The importance of human connections between clients and their advisers will always be essential'."[63]

---

59 "PWM/The Banker Private Banking Awards 2020," https://www.thebanker.com/Awards/Private-Banking-Awards/PWM-The-Banker-Private-Banking-Awards-2020 [accessed November 24, 2021]

60 ,"KBC Best Private Bank in Belgium," *ibidem*.

61 "UBS Best Global Private Bank," *ibidem*.

62 "*BNP Paribas Banque privée France* best private bank in France," *ibidem*.

63 Jeff Busconi, chief operating officer at Bank of America Private Bank, "Bank of America Private Bank Best Private Bank in North America for Customer Service," *ibidem*. See: Camille Herlin-Giret, *Rester riche. Enquête sur les gestionnaires de fortune et leurs clients*, Lormont, Le Bord de l'Eau, "Documents," 2019.

6. Final assessments

Despite these incursions into assets and wealth management, and even a few direct investments, both Lazard and Rothschild houses appear specialized in M&A and financial advice, whereas Edmond de Rothschild bank stays focused on quite contrary strategic segments, mainly asset and wealth management. Whilst big banks evolve towards a business model diversified into the main aspects of market banking (derivatives market and clearing, securitization/*titrisation*, rates markets, trading, etc., essentially in London and New York), they stuck to their strategic basis, as a fruit of the "legacy of finance." They belong to the core of French investment banking community,[64] but they still focus on key business fields and thus they keep a quite smaller dimension: willows in size and employed funds, but not in conceptual action ...

Most important pieces of their strength are immaterial advantages edges: due to the high quality and fine-tuned services, the brand-name stays a reference; the "franchise" does mean relevant advice to institutional, capitalist and individual customers. Even if big universal banks, either French or Anglo-Saxon, do deliver trustful contributions, their very "universal" dimension deprives them from the "chic" reference brought by the *Haute Banque* houses.

These latter stay far from their competitors in asset and wealth management, but the effect of size and economies of scale are not their main objectives – and there lies the "legacy" of ancient and historical *Haute Banque* and merchant banking, even if members of families (at Rothschild and Edmond de Rothschild) and the tradition of durable high-level partnerships had to cede room to a few hundreds of europeanized and globalized managerial elites, themselves supported by talented analysts, negotiators and advisers. Their footprint might be designed as a subtle mix of historical practices, relationship business culture, connected experience, partnership spirit, and osmosis with business lawyers and analysts to provide the relevant advice – and to get the best commissions and fees; and at the end bonus and option shares.

[64] See: Michel Fleuriet (PhD from Wharton School, professor at HEC, chairman of Merrill Lynch France then of HSBC France), *Banques d'investissement et de marché. Les métiers des banques d'affaires*, Paris, Économica, 2007.

> "I visit the boss: which strategy, identification of targets, feasibility, contacts, negotiations, achievements; we make quite from the beginning to the end, contrary to the classic bankers. When we are a senior banker, it is necessary to assume the marketing by seeing several customers a day, then we send teams of specialists. There are several practices of business banker's job. Most are general practitioners who maintain a relationship of trust, honesty, reactivity and availability, in addition to the skills. We call on then to specialists to move forward in the case. Or we have the model of the French multi-specialist, such as F. Henrot (bank, insurance, distribution, telecom) or David Dautresme (*associé-gérant* at Lazard in 1997–2000), who want to be unbeatable on several sectors, four or five. Other types of bankers exist: we have the banker psycho-analyst, endowed with an exceptional talent to create an exceptional relation with the customer, such Bruno Roger or Grégoire Chertok. This type of banker begins by saying that the problem is much more complicated, that it is necessary to discuss the feasibility, the available teams in the company customer, where from the necessity of a relation on several years. Another model is the one of the banker coach, who pushes resolutely into action, such as Alain Minc."[65]

One essential advantage edge is the permanence of senior and partner bankers, conversely with big banks where, along the climate of business, budgetary cuts into staff are a frequent practice and where the volatility is somewhat commonplace. Another one is to be found in the mindsets of family or company leadership: in both cases, people in charge, rather to avoid "all-under-the-same-roof" philosophy, as proposed by universal banks, have better to divide their connections, and, in our case study, to entertain "relation banking" with *Haute Banque* houses, and even little boutiques.

65 Interview with an investment banker at Rothschild, 2017.

Tab. 8. Rothschild and Lazard Limited activities

	Rothschild (millions euros)			Lazard (millions $)
	April 2015–March 2016	March–October 2016		2016
	Turnover (commissions, etc.)		Returns	
Financial advices	1.040	537	71	1.301
Among which :				
M&A and other advisory				1.031
Restructuring				202
Wealth management and asset management	379	180	47	
Asset management				1.031
Capital-investment and private debt	107	73		
Others	63			

Sources: Étienne Goetz, "Rothschild & Co profite du dynamisme du M&A," *Les Échos*, June 23, 2016. Anne Drif, "Rothschild & Co renforce ses positions aux États-Unis," *Les Échos*, November 30, 2016 ; *Lazard Ltd reports full-year and fourth quarter 2016 results*, p. 31

Some analysts even speak of the desire to avoid the conflicts of interests that could take shape within big banks, as each division is supposed to be promoted by its sister ones, perhaps at the expense of the customer … The markets of M&A, underwriting, asset management and wealth management cannot therefore be reduced to oligopolies, despite the size of big banks and their grip over international banking – but even lighter houses like Rothschild and Lazard are challenged by the boutiques.

The "legacy of finance" has therefore been preserved, revitalized, extended thanks to Lazard and Rothschild. "There had been two traditions in Paris, the Jewish bank and the Protestant bank. But that latter disappeared (Hottinguer, Mallet, Vernes, Mirabaud, Neuflize),"[66] even if NSM survived with the ABN-AMRO group and Jean-Philippe Hottinguer succeeded recently to pick bank the *Hottinguer* name to restart some entity. This led to the rebirth (Rothschild) and re-development (Lazard) of two houses that had been set up by Jewish entrepreneurs

66 Interview with a senior investment banker, April 2017. Readers have to understand that several bankers accept an interview only if his/her name is not quoted.

and managed by some of them (M. David-Weill, Édouard and David de Rothschild) in the 1980s–1990, before a new Rothschild generation shared the helm recently.

Beyond these religious topics, the very durability of both houses might seem somewhat amazing, and this could explain the certitudes and pride diffused by some texts, for example by Lazard: "Lazard provides advisory clients with a quality of service we believe no other firm can match. Our client relationships are built on trust and discretion. We are deeply established in business centres around the world, with meaningful local relationships and insight. And as the world's largest advisory-focused firm, we have exceptional depth of expertise across industry sectors and geographies. Our clients are leaders of business and government. They rely on Lazard for sound judgment, discretion, and global scale to address their most challenging assignments."[67]

But merchant houses are being challenged by the very teams of their clients dedicated to finance and law, acting themselves as almost *banquiers d'affaires* and *avocats d'affaires*: this demands therefore more acute skills to face their high levels, and operating modus sticking to secrecy against leaks on the marketplace – which explains for instance that Total prepared its bid on Maersk Petroleum in Summer 2017 by relying first on its internal experts by fear of leaks …

Last one has to consider one hot issue, that of gender, because a solid "invisible ceiling" deprived for long the ladies to climb up the ladder. But steps were steadily reached by pioneers, among whom emerging "female stars." At Lazard Paris in 2017, even if Virginie Morgon left to become CEO of Eurazeo, associates Michèle Lamarche, Alexandra Soto (at the London bureau), Amélie Negrier (in Chicago) or Isabelle Xoual have emerged. It is also the case of Yan Lan, the head of Lazard in China (Beijing, Hong Kong, Taiwan), who drifted from a high job at Gide law cabinet to join Lazard in 2011 and supervise the Chinese M&A market. On her side, Anne-Laure Kiechel, at Rotshchild, became an acute specialist in advice to foreign States: this *associée-gérante* supervised for example the Greek debt exchange in November 2017 (25 billion €) or, in December 2017, the Argentina plan to finance infrastructures (30 billion $), through PPP investments raised on several market places.

---

67 Lazard institutional communication, 2017.

Finally, the overall issues are the capacity to resist competition and volatility and to maintain the capital of durability, as the *VUCA* matrix questions it (Tab. 9):

Tab. 9. VUCA matrix about investment and merchant banking

Volatility • Dependance of the M&A market on geopolitics and geo-economics • Permanent risks of turnover among key partners Betting on the capital of competence of family inheritors? And of juniors' ability to equalize bigwigs in partnerships	Uncertainties • Fate of interests' rates along the policies of central banks, with the effects on the activity of asset management • Tensions within families or within partnership about business models Rivalries among the Rothschild branches
Competition • How far will business units by big universal banks equal *Haute Banque* teams (wealth management, M&A, financial advice)? • Would it remain possible to escape businesses like securitization (*titrisation*)? • Will the upsurge of the rules of transparency reduce the room for manoeuvre of wealth managers?	Ambiguities • Embeddedness on one marketplace or europeanization or globalization? *Haute Banque roots* vs national cultural legacy or multiculture? • What scope for the diversification? What kind of strategy and business model? • What about ladies within partnerships? What about the gender gap (along the model of Anne-Laure Kiechel, at Rotshchild in the wake of Virginie Morgon, from Lazard and now CEO of Eurazeo)?

Panel discussion: Incubators of banking innovation

The panel discussion took place in June 2017 and reflects the thoughts of the participants at that time. When it comes to banking and fintech innovation, we know that change is fast and we need to bear this in mind when looking back at this debate.

Participants:

David El Nouchi (ClubFunding)

Yassin Hankir (savedroid / Advanced Bitcoin Technologies)

Anne-Cécile Lugagne-Delpon (BNP Paribas Wealth Management France)

Bernhard Obenhuber (SWISS FIN LAB)

Jean-Michel Pailhon (Ciallogy/ESSEC/Panthéon-Assas University, Paris)

Arash Sorouchyari (Lombard Odier)

Moderator: Hugo Bänziger (Chairman of EABH).

Hugo Bänziger introduced the topic under discussion by the panel: putting into perspective the innovations and contributions of *Haute Banque*, we will look at the transformations and disruptions of finance today and in particular the contribution of fintechs.

He asked the panel members to introduce themselves: David El Nouchi is the CEO of ClubFunding, a crowdfunding platform that enables the issuance of bonds for SMEs or VSEs; Yassin Hankir is the CEO of savedroid, a fintech specialized in automatic gamified micro savings; Anne-Cécile Lugagne-Delpon works on digital transformation and innovation within BNP Paribas Wealth Management. Bernhard Obenhuber works in Switzerland on customer data, rating automation and builds algorithms for discretionary portfolio management; Jean-Michel Pailhon teaches at the University of Pantheon-Assas and, with his company Ciallogy, works in particular on blockchain and crypto currencies; Arash Sorouchyari works within Lombard Odier on a portfolio management system (GX project) and pushes innovation inside the bank so that it is as disruptive as if it came from an outside company.

Hugo Bänziger: What are the shortcomings of the financial system today that explain the success of fintechs?

Jean-Michel Pailhon thinks that fintechs are tackling problems that are at niche level, especially in real estate and mortgage lending, which has a significant impact on banks' balance sheets. There are many players trying to disrupt this market, especially in the US and the UK; it is a complex market because the capital requirements are high. For this reason, it is still mainly in the hands of banks for the time being, which is what we see in France.

For *Yassin Hankir*, the issue today is access to complex financial products. It is a question of inclusion, on two levels: on the one hand, it is about giving access to the unbanked public in the least developed countries, and on the other hand, it consists in offering private banking advice at a lower cost, thanks to robots, advice that was only accessible to high net worth individuals (HNWI) until now. It is therefore mainly a question of democratizing financial services and starting from the user's needs, breaking with the practice of banks which, until now, thought too much in terms of products and processes. Fintechs are taking advantage of this favourable situation by starting from scratch, whereas traditional banks have to manage a legacy. By simplifying the process, costs can be lowered, hence a robo-advisor charges a fee of about 0.7 % for asset management, compared to 2.5 to 3 % in the traditional system.

Bernhard Obenhuber confirms this trend to be customer centric. The knowledge of customers that banks used to have has weakened. Today, social networks and other platforms have a much better view on consumer preferences and interests. FinTechs try to combine personal data from various sources with the traditional banking data. However, FinTechs need to work with traditional banks to unlock the full potential.

Hugo Bänziger: How do the representatives of the classical banks receive these criticisms, especially for not being customer centric?

For *Arash Sorouchyari*, these criticisms are justified in some respects, but the situation varies from one bank to another. Banks have been subject to massive regulations in recent years, thus focusing most of their tech effort on their implementation. This has led to slowness in the digitization process; however, they invest heavily to catch up. Unlike fintechs, they cannot start from scratch and must deal with their existing IT platforms and legacy processes as well. However, fintechs can be an opportunity for them in accelerating the digitization. "In our case, we have put a strong emphasis on the client experience first in the way we provide our business capabilities and then we work on the underlying processes and systems." experience, as Amazon can do.

Anne-Cécile Lugagne-Delpon agrees with this analysis on the need to start from the customer's needs, because these evolve with what companies like Amazon offer them; on the other hand, there is also a regulatory and transparency requirement. Fintechs are challenging banks in terms of time to market by forcing them to work differently than before. What is new is to be able to work with customers, and to design the customer journey with them, and also to work with fintechs.

Hugo Bänziger: Are banks able to adapt to these changes?

For *David El Nouchi*, they don't finance SMEs and VSEs enough, or at least have this often unjustified reputation, and they have a lot of constraints in their business. When the fintech Nickel was acquired in France by BNP Paribas, its reputation among start-ups declined. On the other hand, the constraints that affect banks are opportunities for fintechs in niche markets.

Hugo Bänziger: Some examples of consumer focus? Are banks in capacity to accelerate their processes when there are still many manual phases?

Yassin Hankir indicates that the starting point is to truly understand the user needs, then the process is facilitated by the absence of legacy; finally, it is necessary to engage in a permanent dialogue with the users because preferences and behaviours evolve quickly and it is necessary to adapt fast, which technology allows.

Asked about blockchain, *Jean-Michel Pailhon* explains how it works, indicating that this decentralized virtual registry will be useful for value transfers on complex assets such as derivatives and OTCs, but has so far proved to be unprofitable for dealing in equity. However, the REPO market will be improved for example and many proofs of concept are currently being tested. He believes that we are going to experience a revolution similar to that of the internet in the early 2000s.

For *Arash Sorouchyari* the client onboarding is clearly one of the important customer focused touch points at Lombard Odier. For HNWI and UHNWI the process is much more complex than for a classic saving account. The existence of some legacy systems in banks makes the digitization of such processes more complex; however, the true challenge is to really rethink the end-to-end process and not just digitize the old way of opening the accounts.

Anne-Cécile Lugagne-Delpon indicates that the first project was the onboarding of the new customer, which is a nightmare for the customer and the banker. The customer journey was redesigned with fintech, using artificial intelligence. "Depending on the customer's profile, we could have 100 to 200 contracts and we managed to reduce that to a few clicks." She also emphasizes the importance of change management among employees, even when it comes to automating low-value-added tasks. Two initiatives help to accelerate innovation: submitting a project to several selected fintechs, and a hackaton in various places of the Group in the World.

Hugo Bänziger: What products do the fintechs offer?

David El Nouchi's firm is specialized in crowd lending, allowing to democratize access to capital for very small companies in a very short time. For investors, the return is as high (around 10 %) as what large groups can offer to powerful investors.

Bernhard Obenhuber works on data protection for banks and companies (not on the retail market), especially in the context of the GDPR: he enables his clients to be compliant with the regulation but also to use data and thus use the regulation as a catalyst.

Hugo Bänziger: What will be the legacy of the current financial system in 50 years?

For *Yassin Hankir*, the big change will be technology, which allows aggregation, analysis, with a stronger presence of robo-advisors to precisely define the needs of the client. Automation will transform retail banking, where margins are very low, which will lead to a shrinking of the traditional banking sector.

David El Nouchi believes that banks are using fintechs to outsource their innovation (as we also see in the pharmaceutical industry, for example); after a natural selection, the best start-ups will be bought by the banks.

Jean-Michel Pailhon does not want to risk a 50-year forecast but believes that the universal bank will not survive in favour of platforms allowing to buy not by producers but by products or services. However, he believes that when it comes to money, the mindset remains the need for security and a minimum of human relations, which excludes full digital.

For *Bernhard Obenhuber*, trust is fundamental for both money and data and there is no reason why banks should not be well positioned in the future as they have been in the past.

Arash Sorouchyari believes that the democratization of services will expand the business; however, banks have to reinvent themselves with the pressure on costs and prices, as new generations are used to getting and using many free services. Banks will have to favour a more platform & ecosystem-based approach to provide their clients with a more holistic set of services and experiences.

Anne-Cécile Lugagne-Delpon wishes to nuance and qualify the vision of the robo-advisors: as banks continue to have the money and the customers, fintechs are not breaking through in the business to consumer

(BtoC); it is rather the BtoBtoC (business to business to consumer). She perceives a more important disruption in the emerging countries, like in Africa, where they are skipping some development steps and where telecom stores for payments are flourishing more than bank branches.

Arash Sorouchyari agrees and emphasizes the need for the right balance of human touch and digital capabilities compared to robo-advisors. The importance of the human touch is to bring new perspectives to clients and support them during stressful events such as the financial crisis like the one we had. In such cases, customers need to turn to a human advisor for explanation and support and the robo-advisors reach their limits.

Hugo Bänziger: Centralization, decentralization: which interface for the customer in the future?

For *Yassin Hankir,* big techs will be the essential intermediaries because they hold the distribution channels, i.e., the last mile towards the user. He also believes that the younger generations believe in technology and thus, will rely on it more confidently and easily. We should therefore see more specialization on banking products to reduce costs as well as centralization to achieve economies of scale.

Arash Sorouchyari believes that tech companies don't want to do banking and get bogged down with regulatory issues but they will position themselves between the customer and the bank for very focused and specific retail activities.

Jean-Michel Pailhon points out that GAFA are not interested in the banking industry because they would have the cash to buy any banking giant and they don't. Their goal is to keep the customer on their platforms as long as possible and offer services such as payments; Facebook has thus put the former head of PayPal at the head of Messenger to implement a payment system in the messaging system.

Anne-Cécile Lugagne-Delpon agrees and believes that regulation, which is a burden for banks, is also a protection for them because of the barriers to entry it creates.

David El Nouchi thinks that big tech will invest in the financial sector for payments, as we are already seeing, but also for crowd funding, which interests Facebook; however, there will remain niches where quality and human relations will prevail.

Bernhard Obenhuber is convinced that banks will remain even if the size of the banking industry decreases; they could also transform themselves into custodians not only of financial assets but also of personal data.

Concluding remarks

Youssef Cassis

In these concluding remarks, I would like to address some of the issues raised in this book, as well as the conference from which it originates, in a historical and comparative perspective.[1] I will first address the question of the definition of the *Haute Banque*, and then consider its main functions; its rise, decline, the question of its possible re-emergence; and finally its significance for long-term economic and financial development.

1. Defining the *Haute Banque*

What is the *Haute Banque*? The question has been raised on a number of occasions, especially by Jacques de Larosière, Nicolas Stoskopf and Laure Quennouëlle-Corre, but it is important to come back to this central issue. In the first place, the *Haute Banque* must be defined simultaneously in economic, social and political terms. At economic level, it consisted of a group of family-owned private banks – in other words, their owners were also their managers; they were usually called partners, *associés* in French. These banks were engaged in the most prestigious banking and financial activities: merchant banking (financing of international trade), investment banking (issuing of foreign loans, whether on behalf of foreign governments or large corporations); and private

1 In addition to the papers presented at the conference on "The legacy of the *Haute Banque* in the world. From the 19th to the 21st century", these remarks are based on my book, jointly written with Philip Cottrell, *Private Banking in Europe. Rise, Retreat, and Resurgence*, Oxford, Oxford University Press, 2015. See also Youssef Cassis, "Private banks and private banking," in Youssef Cassis, Richard Grossman and Catherine Schenk (eds.), *The Oxford Handbook of Banking and Financial History*, Oxford, Oxford University Press, 2016, p. 87–109.

banking (managing the funds of wealthy customers, originally their own and those of their relatives).

At social level, the members of the *Haute Banque* were very wealthy and fully integrated into their country's upper classes, whether the landed aristocracy or the upper middle classes, the *haute bourgeoisie* or *grande bourgeoisie*. At the same time, many of them had foreign origins, belonged to religious minorities, mainly Jewish and Protestant, and were part of international networks of relationships, at business, family, and religious levels – the Rothschilds are the best but in no way the only example of such networks.

Finally, the *Haute Banque* was close to political power, mainly in an advisory capacity, whether in its home country or in the foreign countries for which *Haute Banque* houses acted as financial agents and representatives. Their members thus enjoyed a combination of economic power, social prestige, and political influence. This means that the *Haute Banque* was a very exclusive group, made up of only a handful of banking houses (half a dozen, maybe a little more), within the world of private banks. It is important to bear in mind that there is no official list of its members: members simply knew that they belonged to this exclusive group, which was perceived as such, in its broad contours, by the outside world.

Within these general characteristics, this common denominator, one could distinguish between a narrow and a broad definition of the *Haute Banque*. The narrow definition applies to the Parisian *Haute Banque*. It was, after all, within the specific Parisian context that the concept was formed. The broad definition applies to the banking aristocracy of other leading financial centres, in the first place London and New York.

2. The Parisian *Haute Banque*

The Parisian *Haute Banque* took shape during the *Restauration*, between 1815 and 1830, with the arrival in Paris of a number of French provincial banks (Perier, Seillière, Fould), followed by Swiss ones, several already present in the capital under the *Ancien Régime* (Mallet, Perregaux, Delessert, Hottinguer), and then by German ones, first of all the Rothschilds. The Parisian *Haute Banque* enjoyed its golden age between 1830 and 1870. Its pre-eminence in international finance reached its peak in 1871–1872, with the issue of the two war indemnity loans, following France's defeat against Prussia in 1871. Thereafter, an increasing share of the foreign loans issued in France was handled by the newly created commercial and investment banks, including the Banque de Paris et des Pays-Bas, established on the initiative of the *Haute Banque* in 1872. With the exception of the Rothschilds, who remained an immense financial power until 1914, the other members of the Parisian *Haute Banque* became progressively marginalized.

However, they still played a role out of proportion with the size of their firms. Their prestige and network of relationships gave them a competitive edge in such fields as private portfolio management, which had become their main activity by the early 20th century. They also partly remained bankers to foreign governments and they were strongly represented on the boards of the *banques d'affaires* (especially the Banque de l'Union parisienne, which they created in 1904), the major insurance and railway companies and among the *regents* (directors) of the Banque de France.

It could be said that the Parisian *Haute Banque* lost a great deal of economic power, but retained a fair amount of social prestige and political influence. Including the Rothschilds, it continued to decline during the interwar years, and only retained a symbolic presence within the French banking system after the Second World War, despite a revival of firms such as Rothschild or Lazard in the last third of the 20th century, as pointed out by Hubert Bonin.

3. London's and New York's *Haute Banque*

Interestingly, just as the Parisian *Haute Banque* was starting its inexorable decline, another group of private bankers was rising to even greater prominence, first and foremost in London, and then in New York – the two leading international financial centres of the 20th century. In my view, such prestigious banking houses should definitely be included in a geographically broadened notion of the *Haute Banque*. They could be described by the French term *Haute Banque* – I have personally tended to do so – but the concepts of banking aristocracy or, though to a lesser extent, High Finance, could also be applied.

A mainly home-grown banking aristocracy was already established in London by the early 19th century: the partners of the so-called London private banks, which were primarily deposit banks, best exemplified by such figures as Samuel Jones-Loyd, 1st Baron Overstone (1796–1883), or George Grenfell Glyn, 2nd Baron Wolverton (1824–1887). They were to disappear in the last third of the 19th century as a result of the amalgamation movement in English banking.

On the other hand, the late 19th and early 20th century was a true golden age for the private banks engaged in international finance, in other words the London merchant banks. Far from declining or simply resisting the trend towards consolidation, they expanded enormously the scale of their activities, taking advantage of the pivotal role played by the City of London in the growth and globalization of the world economy. Merchant banks were able to maintain their hold on the huge London accepting and issuing businesses, which were at the heart of London's position as the world's leading financial centre. This was possible because of their expertise and networks of international relations, but also because of the highly specialized nature of the English banking system, which limited competition from the far larger English and foreign commercial banks.

The most prominent houses (Rothschilds, Barings, Schroders, Morgans, Kleinwort, Hambros, and a few others) thus retained a considerable amount of economic power, alongside their social prestige – they had been educated in the leading public schools, such as Eton, Winchester, or Harrow, and were fully integrated through intermarriages into the landed aristocracy – and political influence – they were regularly consulted – well into the 20th century, by the British as well as foreign governments over domestic and international financial matters.

In New York, the leading investment banks (JP Morgan, Kidder Peabody, Lee Higginson, Kuhn Loeb, Speyer, Seligman, and a few others) retained an equally strong position in investment banking – the issuing, distributing, and trading of securities. Their economic power, or suspicions about excessive economic power, led to the appointment in 1912 of the Pujo commission, to investigate the existence of a "money trust." They were an integral part of New York's upper classes and more than any other house, JP Morgan epitomized the connections between finance and politics.

The London and New York *Haute Banque* retained a fair amount of economic power until the 1970s – in other words nearly a century longer than its Parisian counterpart. In London, the merchant banks successfully turned to domestic corporate finance to compensate the collapse of international capital flows from the 1930s to the 1960s. In New York, the Glass-Steagall Act protected investment banks from the threat of commercial banks' competition. Their social prestige and political influence were shaken by the financial crises of the Great Depression, without, however, being eradicated.

Things started to change from the 1960s, with the conversion of most merchant banks and investment banks into public companies. A number of conversions had taken place earlier – as early as 1890 for Baring Brothers. What changed in the 1960s was the opening of both ownership and control, on a large scale, to outside interests. This meant the end of the private bank character of these venerable institutions – an essential requirement to be considered as a *Haute Banque* house – and ultimately led to their being taken over by large universal banks – in other words to their disappearance.

It thus makes sense, in my view, to adopt a broad definition of the *Haute Banque*, in order to properly understand its functions, the phases of its rise and decline, and its economic significance. However, I would limit my broader definition to the banking aristocracy of the world's leading financial centres, which played a truly global role. Berlin could have been included between 1870 and 1914. Nevertheless, its leading private members, Bleichröder, Mendelssohn and a couple of others were, as in Paris, marginalized by the large credit banks and never enjoyed the collective power and prestige of their Parisian counterparts.

As for the banking elite of other financial centres, they can be considered as forming a *Haute Banque* at a local rather than a global level, because of the limited size and influence of the financial centres from which they operated – Frankfurt, Hamburg, Amsterdam, Brussels, Zurich, or Geneva – or their peripheral character: Vienna or Saint-Petersburg before 1914.

4. The disappearance of the *Haute Banque*

What have been the consequences of the disappearance of the *Haute Banque*? This is my second point. As far as their business activities are concerned, there has hardly been any change. Both investment banking and private banking have continued to thrive. They have actually expanded considerably in the twenty years or so preceding the financial debacle of 2008 and have resumed after the initial shock.

But of course the *Haute Banque* cannot be considered solely in terms of its financial activities. Equally if not more important is the socio-economic status of the members of its constituent parts. Here the changes have been more significant. Members of the *Haute Banque* who were partners in a private investment bank were risking their own capital. For their part, the new star investment bankers in the large universal banks have been risking other people's money. And yet the latter, who are salaried managers, have been enjoying many of the privileges of the former, who were owner-managers – especially in terms of remuneration. This was a first in history (there were a few precedents in New York in the 1920s), and there can be little doubt that it was one of the causes of the financial debacle of 2008.

Should the demise of the *Haute Banque* be considered as the end of 'relationship banking', as suggested by Niall Ferguson with reference to Sigmund Warburg, a latecomer to the London *Haute Banque*?[2] The answer is no. "Relationship banking" has been practised by both banks' owner-managers and by banks' salaried managers since the beginning of modern banking in the mid-19th century. Relationship banking could be considered as the trademark of a bank-oriented financial system (in Germany and other continental European countries), arm-length banking as the trademark of a market-oriented one (in the first place Britain and the United States) – though the distinction between the two can be somewhat over-simplistic. Personal relationships with customers tended to be stronger in the *Haute Banque* and more generally in private banks than in joint-stock banks, but were in no way an exclusive attribute of the *Haute Banque*. From this perspective, the demise of private investment banks only played a marginal role in the outbreak of the financial crisis of 2008.

5. Re-emergence of the *Haute Banque*?

Is the *Haute Banque* likely to re-emerge? And should a possible re-emergence be seen positively? The answers to both questions is no – unless you define any wealthy banker risking his or her own capital as a member of the *Haute Banque*.

---

2 Niall Ferguson, "The People's Banker," *Financial Times*, June 26, 2010.

Two essential characteristics of the *Haute Banque*, its prestige and reputation, have been built over a long period of time – at least two generations. The old families of the French, British, or American *Haute Banque* are in no position to remerge at the helm of international investment banking. Hedge funds or private equity managers cannot be considered as forming a new *Haute Banque* – at any rate for the time being. And reintroducing partnerships in investment banking, as has been advocated by some in the wake of the financial debacle of 2008, won't result in the formation of a new *Haute Banque* either, at any rate in the short to medium-term.

Such a move might be a way to avoid future problems, but it hardly seems a realistic option, except for some firms in specialized niches. Rather than attempting to restore the world of private banks that made up the *Haute Banque*, avoiding the excesses of the early 2000s would be better achieved by moving investment banking decidedly away from the remains of the *Haute Banque* – especially in terms of remuneration.

6. The economic significance of the *Haute Banque*

This is not the place for a full assessment of the economic significance of the *Haute Banque*, especially its contribution to economic development. One point, however, should be highlighted as a last concluding remark to the worldwide legacy of the *Haute Banque*: its innovative capacity.

Since the early stages of banking and financial activities, private bankers have been at the root of most financial innovations. Think of the use of bills of exchange in 14th century Italy, the issue of banknotes in 17th century England, the emergence of the 'new bank' in 19th century Europe, or the advent of the Euromarkets in 20th century London, to give but a few examples.

This is a remarkable achievement, though maybe not as surprising as it might first appear. It should not be forgotten that until the second third of the 19th century, private banks were the only existing type of banks, and thus the only ones in a position to innovate. As for the more recent period, we know that small, lean firms have historically proved more innovative and more enterprising than large, bureaucratic ones, and this also applies to the financial innovations of late twentieth and early 21st century. Financial innovation should not be seen as a legacy of the sole *Haute Banque*. It is a far broader phenomenon. Only a minority of the small, personally or family owned and managed, and highly innovative banking and financial firms have belonged to this exclusive but now extinct club.

Index (People and Companies)

About the authors

Hugo Bänziger is the chairman of the European Association for Banking and Financial History (EABH) and Assembly member of the International Committee of the Red Cross. Previously he was a Partner at Lombard Odier (2014–2018), a Finance professor at the University of Chicago (2013) and a Member of the Management Board of Deutsche Bank (2006–2012) where he was responsible for Risk, Treasury, Capital Management and Legal/Compliance. Hugo holds a Doctorate from the University of Berne in Economic History.

Hubert Bonin is a researcher in modern economic history at Sciences Po Bordeaux and at Bordeaux Sciences Economiques/Bordeaux School of Economics Research Centre at Bordeaux University. He is a specialist of the history of services companies (Suez canal company, colonial and overseas trading houses and their maritime affiliates), and moreover of French banking history (regional banks; Paris deposit, corporate and investment banks, with several monography books and a few handbooks). He is also a specialist in business history, having co-guided a dozen of research programs about companies, their strategies and practices. Along commissioned missions or academic studies, he is involved in projects about investment banking from the Paris market-place, merchant and trade banking in China, French banking, and entrepreneurship and European business. [boninmoulleau@gmail.com] [website: www.hubertbonin.fr]

Éric Bussière is Professor emeritus at Sorbonne-University, Jean Monnet Chair in the history of European construction. Director of the UMR SIRICE (2012–2016) (Paris 1-Sorbonne University-CNRS), of the LabEx EHNE (2012–2018), member of several scientific councils including the Association for the History of BNP Paribas of which he is president, the Committee for the Economic and Financial History of France (CHEFF), the Georges Pompidou Institute of which he is honourary president, administrator of Robert Triffin International. Corresponding member of the Portuguese Academy of History, member of the scientific council of the European Academy of Yuste (Spain). He is also director or co-director of several collections of scientific works at PIE-Peter Lang. He is director of the journal *Histoire, Economie et société (HES)*. His work focuses on the history of international economic relations, the history of banking and the history of European construction. In recent years he has co-directed the European Commission's history programme (3 volumes, OPOCE 2007, 2014, 2019). He is also co-author of books on the European action of François-Xavier Ortoli and José-Manuel Barroso.

Youssef Cassis is Professor at the Robert Schuman Centre for Advanced Studies, European University Institute, Florence, and Director of the European Research Council funded project on '*The Memory of Financial Crises: Financial Actors and Global Risk*'. His most recent books include *Crises and Opportunities. The Shaping of Modern Finance* (Oxford University Press, 2011), and, with Philip Cottrell, *Private Banking in Europe: Rise, Retreat and Resurgence* (Oxford University Press, 2015). He has also recently co-edited, with Jean-Jacques van Helten, *The Legacy of the Global Financial Crisis* (I.B. Tauris, 2021); and, with Catherine Schenk, *Remembering and Learning from Financial Crises* (Oxford University Press, 2021).

Ton de Graaf studied modern and economic-social history at the University of Amsterdam. Since 1991 he is corporate historian of ABN AMRO History Department. He published about bank-historical, business-historical and regional-historical themes. He is chairman of the Association Enterprise and History (Vereniging Bedrijf en Historie) and member of the Advisory Council of Netherlands Economic History Archive (NEHA). In 2012 he took his Ph.D. degree at Utrecht University with a study on the Netherlands Trading Society, a predecessor of ABN AMRO Bank. In 2021 he has retired.

Yassin Hankir, Founder & CEO of Advanced Bitcoin Technologies AG: Yassin is Crypto and FinTech entrepreneur and enthusiast by heart. He is Founder and CEO of Advanced Bitcoin Technologies AG and savedroid AG, Co-Host of the Frankfurt FinTech Meetup, and co-founded vaamo, one of the very first German robo-advisors. Before becoming an entrepreneur, Yassin worked as strategy consultant at McKinsey & Company, Inc. During his consulting career he focused on retail and private banking, especially growth strategies, product development and implementation, as well as marketing and distribution in Europe, the Middle East and Southeast Asia. Yassin holds a master in Economics and a Ph.D. in Finance of Goethe-University Frankfurt.

Jacques de Larosière was Head of the French Treasury, Managing Director of the IMF, Governor of the Banque de France and President of the European Bank for Reconstruction and Development. He is a member of the Institut (Académie des sciences morales et politiques). He has just published *40 ans d'égarements économiques*-40 years of economic misguidance (Odile Jacob, 2021).

Anne-Cécile Lugagne-Delpon is Head of Digital and Offering Projects in Banque Privée BNP Paribas.

David El Nouchi is the co-founder of ClubFunding, the French leading crowdfunding platform specialized in real estate, created in 2014. Formerly, David worked in M&A at Lazard Paris office. He is graduated from ESCP Business School and Paris Dauphine University.

Roger Nougaret, after a first position as curator in the public archives, created and directed several historical banking archive departments at Crédit Lyonnais (1991–2004), Crédit Agricole (2005–2010) and BNP Paribas (2011–2021). He was a member of EABH Academic Council from 1998 to 2021 and he chairs the section of Contemporary History at the Comité des Travaux Historiques et Scientifiques (CTHS) in Paris. He has published articles and books on archival science and on banking history. Roger is an archivist-paleographer, graduate of the Ecole Nationale des Chartes.

Bernhard Obenhuber is managing partner at CountryRisk.io, a platform for country and sovereign risk analysis. Bernhard is also partner at SWISS FIN LAB, a Swiss company that develops applications for data protection management. Bernhard brings 10 years of experience in investment strategy and research for the largest Swiss banks with a strong focus on emerging market fixed income and quantitative modelling. He holds master degrees in economics and finance from the University of Innsbruck and is a CFA charterholder.

Jean-Michel Pailhon is Vice-president at Ledger, the leading company in security solutions for crypto-assets, where he heads the B2B activities: Ledger Enterprise Solutions. Before that Jean-Michel spent 15+ years of experience in the Financial industry, working for Euronext and then the New York Stock Exchange ("NYSE"), where he held various management positions covering finance, strategy, fund management, M&A and IPO. He was a founding member of the French fintech start-ups association (https://francefintech.org/en/) and is a lecturer in finance and strategy at ESSEC Business School and Pantheon Assas University (France).

Laure Quennouëlle-Corre is director of research at the Centre National de la Recherche Scientifique (CNRS) in Paris. Her main fields of research relate to economic and financial modern history in an international perspective. Her current researches are centred on State, Enterprises and Markets in monetary, banking and financial areas including works about public debt in historical perspective, money markets, financial elites, women in the banking sector.

Arash Sorouchiary is Executive Vice President, Head of Wealth Management Solutions Development at Lombard Odier and has more than 20 years of experience in designing wealth management softwares. He is currently the head of Wealth Management Solutions Development at Lombard Odier, where he oversees a team of over 90 engineers. At Lombard Odier, Arash has lead the design and implementation of a portfolio management system called G2. In addition to serving Lombard Odier, the G2 platform is also provided by Lombard Odier to otherfinancial institutions. At present, Arash is focusing on implementing digital initiatives, such as CRM or advisory offerings, in the G2 platform. Arash serves on the Lombard Odier Group Digital Committee as the Co-Chief Digital Officer.Arash holds an MSc. in computer science from the Swiss Federal Institute of Technology in Lausanne (notice as of 2017).

Nicolas Stoskopf, professor emeritus at the université de Haute-Alsace in Mulhouse, has been working on the history of companies and corporations. He notably published a dictionary, *Banquiers et financiers parisiens* (collection Les patrons du Second Empire, Paris, Picard, 2002) and the history of the Crédit industriel et commercial (CIC, 1859–2009) on the occasion of the 150th anniversary of this bank (Paris, La Branche, 2009).

Most of his publications can be found on line at: https://halshs.archives-ouvertes.fr

Lorans Tanatar Baruh is a doctor of history and the Associate Director of Research and Programs at SALT since its foundation in 2011. In 1997, she was involved in setting up the Ottoman Bank Archive and Research Centre, one of the institutions that underpins SALT. She takes an interest in the history of the Ottoman Empire in the 19th and early 20th centuries. Her research and publications mainly cover economic, social and urban history of the city of Istanbul.

David K. Thompson is an assistant professor of history at Sacred Heart University in Fairfield, Connecticut, USA. He is the author of *Bonds of War: How Civil War Financial Agents Sold the World on the Union* (University of North Carolina Press, 2022.)

www.ingramcontent.com/pod-product-compliance
Ingram Content Group UK Ltd.
Pitfield, Milton Keynes, MK11 3LW, UK
UKHW020710041026
15590UKWH00002B/581

9 782875 745507